EXPLORING
TEXTILES
Projects for GCSE

Marleen Morgans

Edward Arnold
A division of Hodder & Stoughton
LONDON BALTIMORE MELBOURNE AUCKLAND

Illustrations by Marleen Morgans

© Marleen Morgans 1988

First published in Great Britain 1988

British Library Cataloguing in Publication Data

Morgans, Marleen
 Exploring textiles.
 1. Textiles – For schools
 I. Title
 677

ISBN 0-340-428260

All rights reserved. No part of this publication may be reproduced or transmitted in any form or by any means, electronically or mechanically, including photography, recording or any information storage or retrieval system, without either the prior permission in writing from the publisher or a licence permitting restricted copying. In the United Kingdom such licences are issued by the copyright Licensing Agency, 33–34 Alfred Place, London WC1E 7DP

Typeset in Linotron Cheltenham Book ITC by Gecko Ltd
Printed and bound in Great Britain for Edward Arnold, the educational, Academic and medical publishing division of Hodder and Stoughton Limited, Mill Road, Dunton Green, Sevenoaks, Kent by **The Eastern Press Limited, London and Reading**

Contents

To the teacher 6

1 Tie-dye and Batik 7

Tie-dye 7
Record keeping 8
Exploring tie-dye 9
Simple experiments 10
Projects using tie-dye 11
Questions 12

Batik 13
Record keeping 14
Exploring Batik 15
Simple experiments 16
Projects using Batik 17
Questions 18

2 Patchwork 19

Record keeping 20
Exploring patchwork 20
Simple experiments 22
Project 1 Skylines
 – wallhanging 23
Project 2 Life in the garden
 – floor cushion 25
Project 3 Patchwork oven gloves 27
Questions 28

3 Soft Sculpture 29

Record keeping 30
Exploring soft sculpture 30
Simple experiments 31
Project 1 Strawberries
 – pin-cushions decoration for gateaux or mobiles 34
Project 2 Cherries
 – decoration for gateaux or appliqued picture 35
Project 3 Gateaux or birthday cake
 – a 'fun object' which, enlarged, could be a cushion 36
Project 4 A bunch of bananas
 – soft toys, ornamental art forms 37
Project 5 Oranges and apples
 – soft toys and small decorative objects 38
Project 6 A hamburger
 – 3-D decorative object, pin cushion 39
Questions 40

4 Texture 41

Record keeping 42
Exploring texture 42
Simple experiments 44
Project 1 The King of Hearts
 – a cushion 45
Project 2 Aerial views
 – a prodded rug using rags 48
Project 3 Heroes
 – a wall hanging 50
Questions 52

5 Knitting 53

Record keeping 54
Exploring hand knitting 54
Simple experiments 56
Project 1 Chain mail
 – a fabric panel or cushion 57
Project 2 Cellular structures
 – garment decoration 59
Project 3 Pebbles and pools
 – a decorative textile hanging 62
Questions 64

To the teacher

Exploring Textiles has been structured so as to provide a basis of creative ideas, which will lead to the completion of assessed coursework and project work using accepted needlework skills.

The book encourages pupils to develop their own ideas along the lines suggested, and will combine the needlework skills previously mastered with principles and concepts learned in their art and craft lessons. I am very aware of the common element in the home economics coursework, and I have tried in each chapter to include projects or project extensions which provide the necessary links. However, each project will not be examining all the examinable skills.

Pupils will need to use their imagination and experiment with fabrics to find the best combinations for use, and the stitching most appropriate to any given effect. This will help them to select suitable materials to ensure a satisfactory completion of their own projects.

Decisions have to be made by pupils, not only at the start of the project, but at all stages of development, so that they have to effectively organise and relate their ideas to practical outcomes. To help achieve this goal, the book has been constructed to give some sense of progression.

In the initial evaluation of a project the following points should be considered and discussed:

- What will be the purpose and function of the finished article?

- Are the fabrics available, will they be suitable and how much will they cost?

- Is the equipment available?

- Has the pupil the necessary skills to complete the project?

A symbol of a folder is shown at appropriate places to prompt pupils to record in their folder all experiments, explorations and steps taken, during a project's completion. Above all, I wish the pupil to produce a functional or aesthetically pleasing product which has given the pupil satisfaction and reward in its completion.

Chapter 1

Tie-dye and Batik

Tie-dye

This is a traditional method of resist dyeing. Beautiful patterns can be made by folding, knotting, binding or pleating certain parts of a fabric before dyeing it, so that the dye is excluded from these parts.

The dyed fabric can be used to make blouses, skirts or scarves. The same process can be used to decorate household articles, tee-shirts and summer tops, or to act as a background for any piece of creative textile work, e.g. applique, embroidery or patchwork.

The variations are endless for both design and colour.

Equipment

- utensils to hold the dyes – plastic buckets or bowls
- a means of rinsing the dyed sample – large plastic bowls
- somewhere to hang samples to drip and dry
- fabrics – pure cotton, cotton organdie, silk or fine linen
- Dylon cold water dyes
- strong thread or string to bind the fabric
- old plastic or wooden spoons

Record keeping

Make a clear presentation of all the stages of your work in your note-book or folder.

To achieve this – things to consider:

1 After any exploration work, or experiments, always note down exactly what you did and record your results.

2 Make a note of the dyes, tools and equipment that you used.

3 After testing, make a note of the most suitable fabrics to use, not only for the craft but for the end result.

4 If you make a garment from your tie-dye or batik samples, sketch the outfit and list all the processes involved in its completion.

5 When you evaluate your project, remember to include an estimation of cost and amount of fabric used.

Exploring tie-dye

Begin your first tie-dye experiments by using pieces of fabric, e.g. from old sheets or pillow cases. This fabric, which has been well washed, dyes well, as all the starch or dressing has been removed.

Cut several pieces of fabric, each approximately 20 cm square. Using this fabric, try some of the following suggestions which are intended to act as a guide for further experiments.

Remember that the techniques vary, but the method of dyeing the fabric remains the same.

Make samples of the following techniques for your folder or your notebook making a note as to how each was produced.

Marbling

1 Take a piece of fabric and bunch it up tightly in your hand, until it is like a ball.

2 Bind a strong thread or fine string round and round it in all directions, and tie it tightly.

3 Place the bound fabric in a prepared dye.

4 Leave it in the dye for about 30 minutes.

5 Remove from the dye and rinse thoroughly in cold water.

6 Leave to partially dry, untie the sample, and iron when still damp.

Folding and binding

Many striking patterns and effects, especially stripes are produced by the folding technique combined with binding.

Knotting

This is one of the easiest and quickest ways of producing a tie-dye texture. Tie the knots in the middle of the fabric first.

Twisting and binding

For a circular pattern, pull the fabric up towards the centre, until it is like a closed umbrella. Give the fabric a slight twist, then bind downwards at intervals.

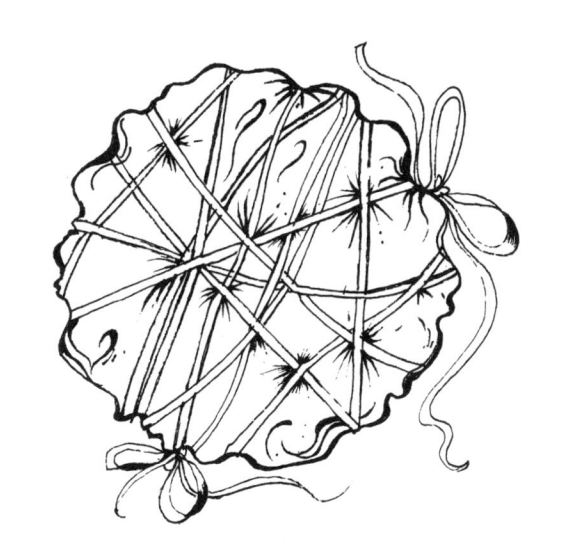

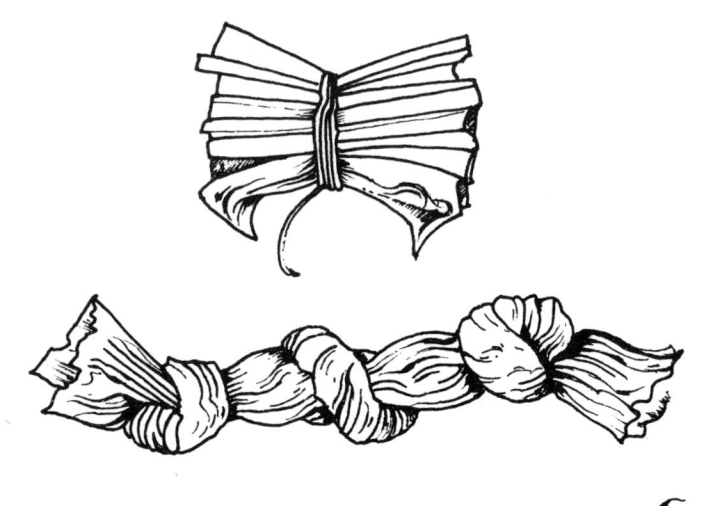

Simple experiments

Make a record of what you did and describe your results in your folder.

1 Vary the length of time you leave the fabric in the dye.

2 Dye a variety of fabrics, other than the ones suggested.

3 Dyes are transparent, and one colour dyed over another will result in a third colour. Experiment on small samples of fabric.

Remember the basic rules of colour mixing.

> red + yellow = orange   red + blue = purple
> yellow + blue = green   purple + orange = brown
> purple + green = grey   violet + blue = indigo
>
> You cannot dye a fabric a lighter colour than it is. You can only dye it darker.

When you have fully explored the techniques involved in tie-dye and have carried out some of the simple experiments, you may like to try some of the projects suggested in the chapter, or tie-dye a length of fabric and make it into a garment. Whatever you choose to do, it is essential at all times to record, present and evaluate your practical work to ensure a successful completion to a project.

Projects using tie-dye

1 Chemical dyes are cheap, easy to use and reliable. However, natural dyes, obtained from natural sources, e.g. onion peelings, blackberries, lichen, tree bark, have their own particular qualities but also have disadvantages.

Explore the possibilities of making your own natural dyes, and using them on your tie-dye samples.

2 If you have a white cotton tee-shirt which you would like to brighten up, try one of the tie-dye techniques on it. Marbling would probably give the most interesting results.

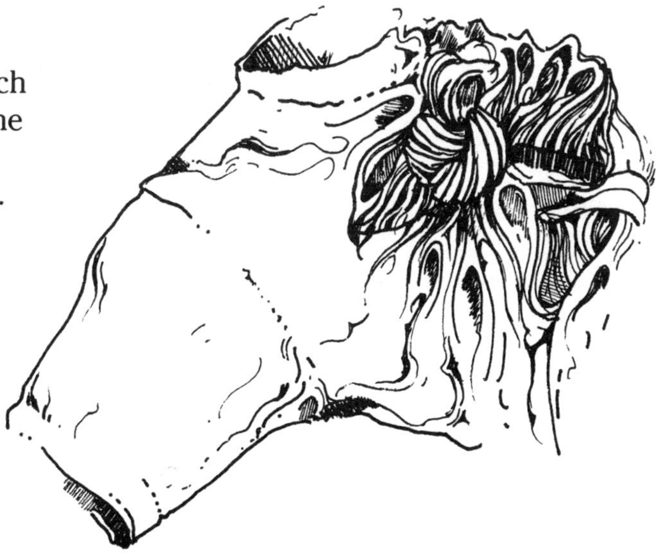

3 Try several tie-dye techniques on one piece of fabric. Choose the most interesting section, and make this the background for a piece of embroidery.

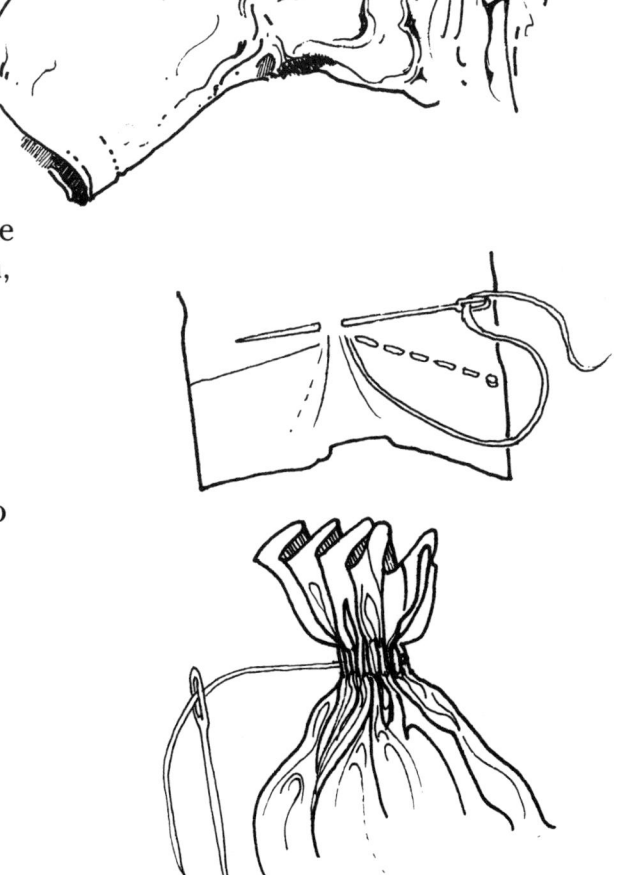

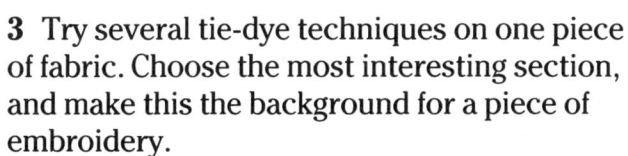

4 Experiment with the sewing method of preparing fabric for tie-dye. This method depends entirely on drawing the material into gathers so closely on the sewing thread that the dye cannot penetrate the folds. It is essential, therefore, to have strong thread. Always start with a large knot, use running stitch, then, for the pulling-up process, gradually slide the fabric along the sewing thread until it is bunched into a solid mass of gathers at one end.

Questions

1 Why do you think it is advisable to wash a tie-dyed item separately?

2 List items of protective clothing which it would be sensible to wear when practising the craft of tie-dye.

3 Why is it advisable to wash a piece of fabric thoroughly before beginning tie-dye?

4 Sketch items of clothing or household articles that you think could be made from the dyed material. If you were to make one of these articles which tie-dye technique do you think would be the most suitable?

Tasks for further study

1 Natural dyes were used to dye all fabric until the middle of the last century. Find out more about natural dyes, their sources and typical colours.
What is the function of a mordant in natural dyeing?

2 The craft of tie-dye has been practised from very early times by people in many different parts of the world. Find out more about its history.

3 Only a few of the tie-dye techniques have been described in this chapter. Find out about other techniques and describe them in your own words with your own diagrams.

4 We know that cotton dyes very well. Find out more about the other properties of cotton.

Batik

This is a resist technique for producing designs on fabric. Briefly, hot wax is applied to selected areas of the fabric. The fabric is then dyed by brushing dye over it or by dipping it into a dye bath. The wax areas repel the dye.

This craft is said to have originated in Java, and is still a major industry there.

Using this method, beautiful decorated fabrics can be made for wall hangings, pillows, cushions, scarves, table cloths and for creating patterned fabric for applique, patchwork and embroidery, as well as for many fashionable items of clothing.

Equipment

- utensils to hold the dyes – plastic bowls or buckets
- a means of rinsing the dyed fabric
- somewhere to hang samples to drip and dry
- fabrics – pure cotton, linen or silk
- Dylon cold water dyes
- a wooden frame to stretch the fabric over (old wooden picture frames are ideal)
- wax – one part beeswax to four parts paraffin wax, or melted down candles
- wax pot
- brushes, blocks and canting tools
- an iron
- newspapers

Record keeping

Even though you will be completing different processes throughout this chapter the planning stages are the same.

For each piece of work you attempt you should include the following in your folder:

1 Sketches of how your original designs developed.

2 Samples of any yarn/fabric tests you made to discover which best suited the purpose.

3 A list of all the equipment you used to complete the article or garment.

4 Sketches/plans of how to make the item.

5 An estimation of cost and amount of yarn/fabric needed to complete the project.

6 Notes on any plans, decisions or choices you had to make during any experimental or investigative work.

7 If dyes were used make a record of the recipe and include any dye tests and samples.

8 Include examples of techniques and sample patterns you have tried or made.

9 Evaluate your project.

Exploring Batik

As with tie-dye, it is advisable to use well washed fabric for experiments. If the cloth feels stiff, wash it in boiling water with soap and detergent to remove the finish.

The method of dyeing the fabric is the same as for tie-dye, but there are many ways in which the hot wax can be applied.

Dropped wax

1 Pin the cloth tightly over a frame, or spread it out on layers of newspapers.

2 Melt the wax in the wax pot until a hazy blue smoke appears. **THIS IS ESSENTIAL FOR GOOD RESULTS BUT GREAT CARE MUST BE TAKEN TO PREVENT ANY ACCIDENTS.**

3 Begin your experiments by simply dropping hot wax from a paint brush in a random fashion over the fabric.

4 When waxing is completed, remove the cloth from the frame and place under a cold water tap, or in a bowl of cold water.

5 Place the cloth in the dye and gently stir it around.

6 When dyeing is complete, remove the fabric and rinse in cold water until the water runs clear.

7 Hang the fabric away from the heat to dry.

9 Remove the wax from the fabric by ironing the fabric with a hot iron between sheets of newspaper. The paper must be changed frequently. Using this method the fabric never really seems to be free of wax.

9 Another method of removing wax is to put the waxed fabric into a bowl of boiling water that contains a detergent. The fabric is moved around gently for three minutes, then removed and placed in cold water. The wax can then be shaken off. Repeat the process until there is no trace of wax left in the cloth. The fabric is then washed in soapy water, rinsed and dried.
NEVER POUR WATER CONTAINING WAX DOWN THE SINK.

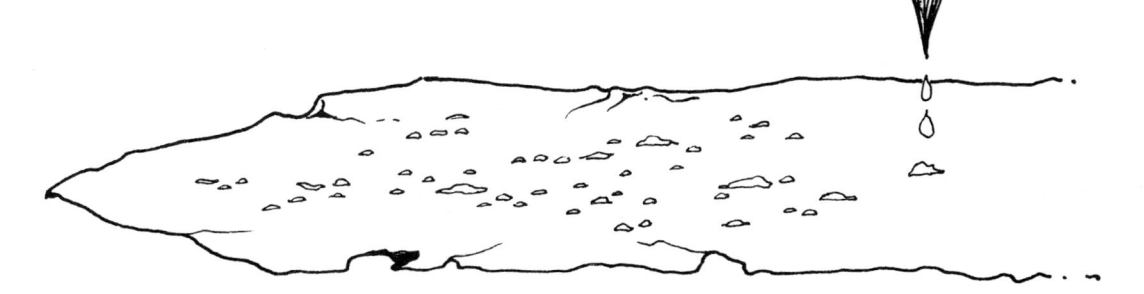

Use some of the following ideas as a guide for further exploration of the craft.

Make samples of the following techniques for your folder, making a note as to how each was produced.

Brushed wax

Ordinary paint brushes can be used to fill in large areas or to make stripes, spots and squares.

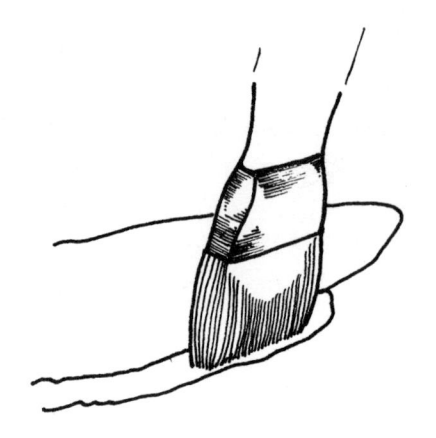

Blocks

Blocks made from knitting needle knobs, wooden bobbins, bolts, nuts, pins stuck in corks or tin cans, can all produce interesting patterns when dipped into hot wax and then pressed onto the fabric.

Canting

A canting tool produces fine lines, circles and dots. The tool is dipped into hot wax to fill the reservoir, then carried to the surface of the fabric. It is advisable to hold a piece of paper under the spout to catch any drips.

It is always a good idea to draw the design onto the fabric with a piece of charcoal before applying the wax, especially if the design is complicated. The charcoal will wash out as the fabric is dipped, rinsed and finally washed.

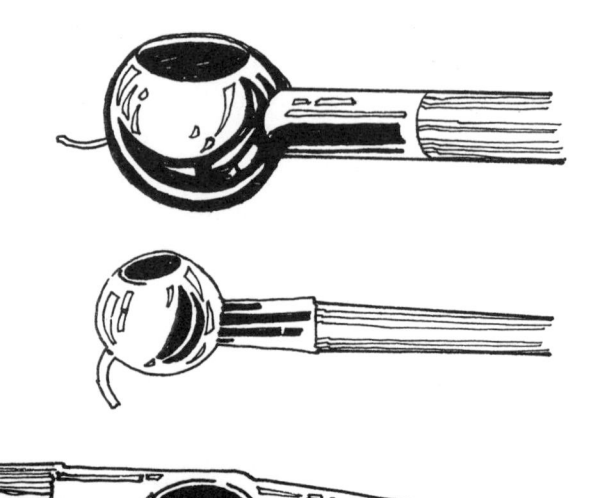

Simple experiments

Make a note of what you did and describe your results so you have a record for your folder.

1 Vary the length of time you leave the fabric in the dye.

2 Dye fabrics other than the ones suggested.

3 Crumple the fabric under cold water long enough to allow the wax to crack before placing the fabric in the dye. Paraffin wax is most suitable for this technique as it is more brittle than beeswax.

4 Explore possible colour combinations. If the fabric is to be dyed with a second colour, cover the areas to remain the first colour with wax and repeat the dyeing process. Refer to the tie-dye section for basic rules on colour mixing.
   When you are confident in using the skills involved with batik, either attempt the following projects, or batik a length of fabric before making it up into a garment.
   Always record, present and evaluate your project.

Projects using batik

1 Try painting the dye directly onto the waxed fabric. Some interesting effects and subtle use of colour can be developed through the use of different brush strokes.

2 Cut six pieces of cotton fabric 35 cm × 25 cm. Decorate each piece with a similar technique and place in a similar dye. Hem around the edges when complete and use as place mats.

3 Other materials beside fabric can be decorated using a similar resist technique. Wax can be used to decorate eggs before placing them in a dye. Doing this is traditional at Easter time in Slavic countries and in some parts of northern England. Wax resist is also used to decorate ceramics. The design is painted on the pot with a wax emulsion which resists the glaze.
   Try to use your school facilities, either your home economics room or art room, to experiment with using wax as a resist.

Questions

1 Why is it necessary to use cold water dyes when experimenting with batik?

2 In Indonesia, where the craft of batik flourishes, wax is applied to both sides of the fabric. What difference do you think this makes to the finished item?

3 List the different ways in which hot wax can be applied to fabric.

4 Draw a diagram of a canting tool and describe how it works.

5 If the wax on the cloth is not hard when the fabric is immersed in dye, the pattern will be spoilt. List ways in which the wax can be hardened.

6 Which liquids, other than wax, poured down a sink could cause a blockage?

Tasks for further study

1 Indonesian batik motifs all have special meanings. Find out more about the history of batik, the influences and the primitive symbols used in the craft.

2 Paste resist is probably the oldest form of batik. Do some research into this ancient technique.

3 Silk is an excellent fabric for batik as it dyes so well. It lends itself to some of the more intricate techniques which are then fashioned into garments. What other properties does silk have?

Chapter 2
Patchwork

Patchwork provides a means of using pieces of material, often cut into geometric shapes using templates, to form a finished product, usually a quilt, cushion, bag or cot cover. The shapes interlock together, and are sewn to form all-over patterns without backgrounds. The final result depends upon the texture, colour and combinations of the materials used.

The art of patchwork probably reached its peak in north America around 1774–1786. The people who settled at that time used every scrap of left over fabric and made it into patchwork quilts to keep themselves warm. These original patchworks were made from randomly cut shapes which were stitched together. This type became known as "crazy patchwork".

In America, patchwork became a Folk art. There are hundreds of traditional American block patterns with wonderful names like Cactus Basket, Dove in the Window, Railroad, Indian Trail, Court House Steps, Log Cabin, Flying Dutchman and Lady of the Lake. By the time they were married girls were expected to have made twelve quilts!

However, a project undertaken in patchwork need not necessarily be a quilt, cushion or cot cover. There is no reason why it should not have a background, and also it need not necessarily consist of only one geometric shape. This allows you to experiment.

Equipment

- closely woven pure cotton, printed or plain
- templates – either plastic, metal or made yourself from thin card
- two pairs of sharp scissors, one for paper and one for fabric
- pins and needles
- threads
- paper backings – made from old cards, envelopes, brown wrapping paper or thin sand paper (this is ideal as it grips the fabric, but is expensive)

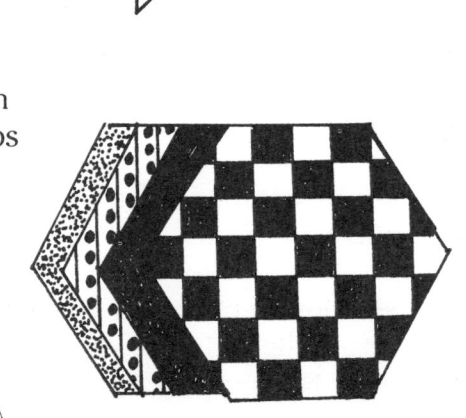

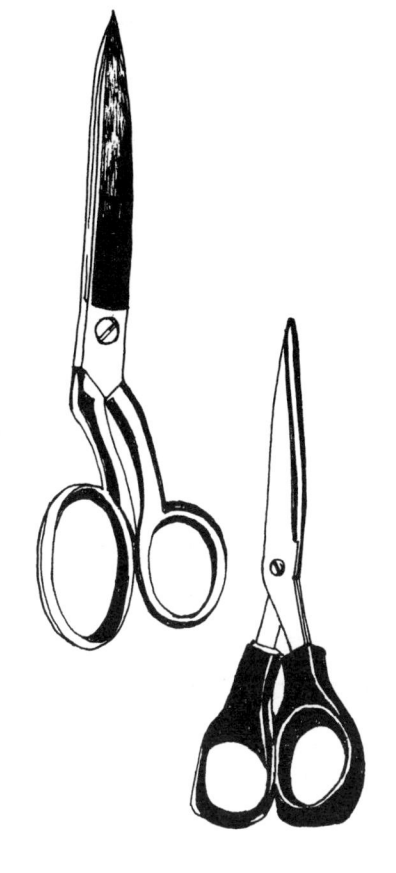

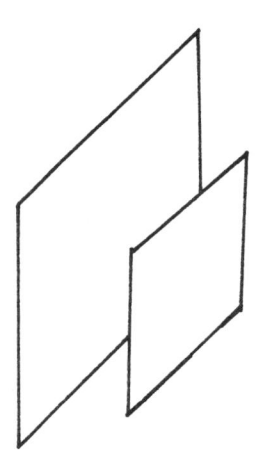

Record keeping

Make a clear presentation of all the stages of your work in your note-book or folder.

To achieve this – things to consider:-

1 After any exploration work, or experiments, always note down exactly what you did and record your results.

2 Make a note of all the tools and equipment that you used.

3 Make a note of the most suitable fabrics to use which fit the purpose of your project, for example – whether or not it will need to be washed frequently or receive hard wear.

4 Show how you developed your original designs for your project.

5 When you evaluate your project, remember to include an estimation of cost and amount of fabric used.

Exploring patchwork

There are three main factors which will contribute to a successful piece of patchwork:

choice of fabric   making a template   folding a corner

If these three factors are ignored, then the result will be disappointing, and a waste of time, effort and material.

Choice of fabric

1 Fabrics should all be the same weight, so that they will lie smoothly when joined together.

2 Avoid crease-resistant synthetic fabrics, stretchy, loosely-woven fabrics, or fabrics that fray.

3 Consider the end result of the fabric, i.e. whether or not it will need to be washed frequently, or receive hard wear.

4 All fabrics should be colour-fast.

5 Make sure that the fabrics have plenty of contrast by mixing different colours, tones, spots, checks and stripes.

Select at random some pieces of fabric from the scrap box. Look at them carefully and try to choose those samples which you think would be suitable for patchwork. Put the samples in your folder.

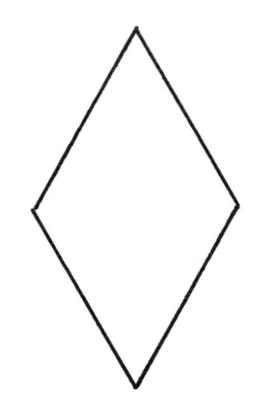

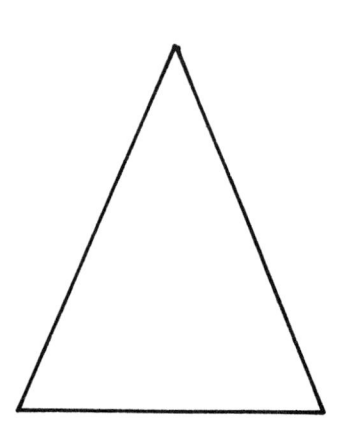

Making a template

Make a template for yourself considering carefully the following points:

1 measure accurately

2 cut precisely, so that all edges are straight

3 have angles which are correctly formed

Template shapes are usually geometric and may include different sizes of hexagons, diamonds, triangles and squares.

Folding a corner

The hexagon is possibly the simplest shape to use as it is the easiest to turn under and join neatly. It is essential to fold the fabric correctly over each corner. The following diagrams illustrate how corners should be folded on hexagons, triangles and diamonds, before tacking and pressing.

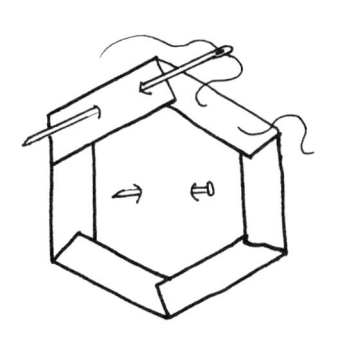

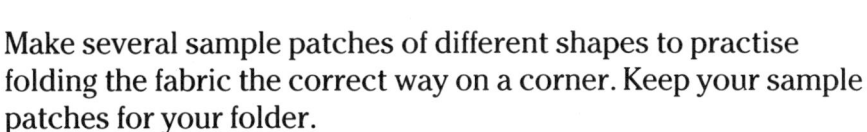

Make several sample patches of different shapes to practise folding the fabric the correct way on a corner. Keep your sample patches for your folder.

Although it is not necessary to use paper backings for fabric patches, it is advisable as the paper helps to retain the shape and firmness of the fabric patches. For a wall hanging, the paper patches can be left in, but should be removed from all work which is likely to be washed. These papers can often help date a piece of patchwork, especially when dated stamps, letters and newspapers have been used.

The diagrams show how the patches are joined together.

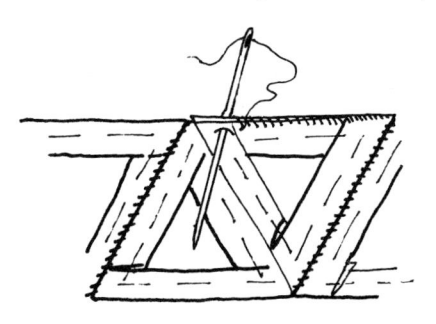

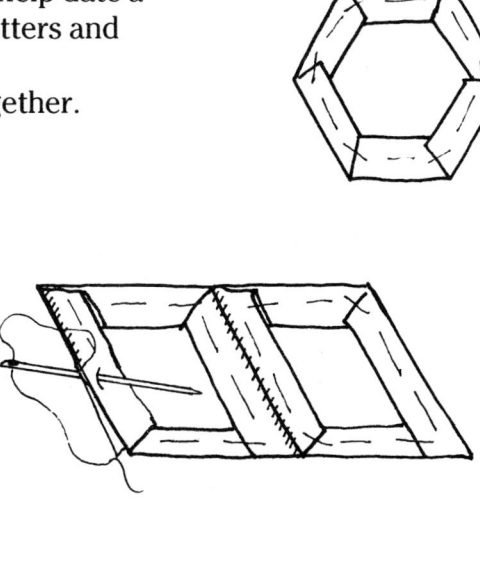

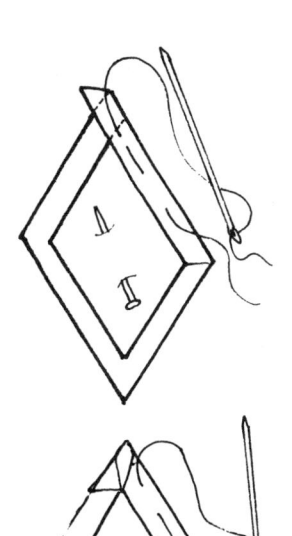

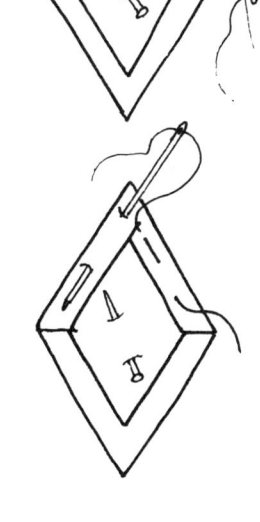

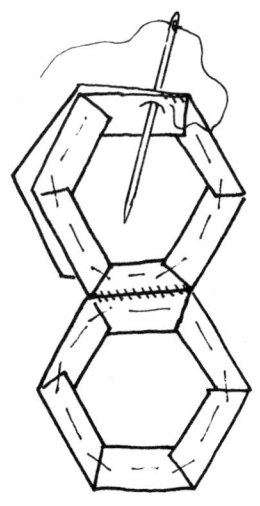

Simple experiments

Make a record of what you did for your folder.

1 Experiment to test for colour-fastness. Select a small piece of fabric that you think is suitable for patchwork, and boil it in detergent together with a small piece of cotton. Record your results.

2 Take a small piece of jersey, which stretches, and mix it with a piece of cotton in a small patchwork sample using a hexagon template. You will discover that the mixture is unsuitable. List your reasons why, and record your results.
Iron the sample and again record your results.

3 Take a piece of each of the fabrics listed:

> hessian, acrilan, coarse linen, gingham

Using a hexagon shaped template, make a patch from each of the pieces of fabric. Record and describe in detail the problems you discover.

4 Tie-dye a piece of white cotton about 40 cm square. Using this make a patchwork using a template shape of your choice. Keep a record of all the skills used and problems encountered in:

> tie-dyeing the cotton
> cutting a template
> making the patches
> joining the patches
> washing the finished article
> ironing the patchwork

List the products which could be achieved by developing the patchwork sample.

Project 1 Skylines
– a wall hanging

Points to consider before starting the project:

> Where will the wall hanging be used?
> Could it be functional as well as decorative?

Suggested uses:
A wall hanging for:

> a foyer or entrance hall of a school
> estate agents office
> architects office
> a draft excluder for a small window

Draw up a design brief considering the following:

> available fabrics
> suitability of fabrics
> colour, size, cost
> equipment available
> production of template and/or pattern and design

Suggested size: 70 cm × 50 cm

Suggested fabric:

> cotton for tie-dye or batik background
> appropriate cotton material for patchwork

Very careful consideration must be given to the size of the patch template and the design you choose, in relation to the size and shape of the end product.

Working hints:

1 Look carefully at buildings silhouetted against a brighter lighter sky.

2 Buildings, roofs, chimneys viewed at a distance or close up, both give a tremendous variety of shapes.

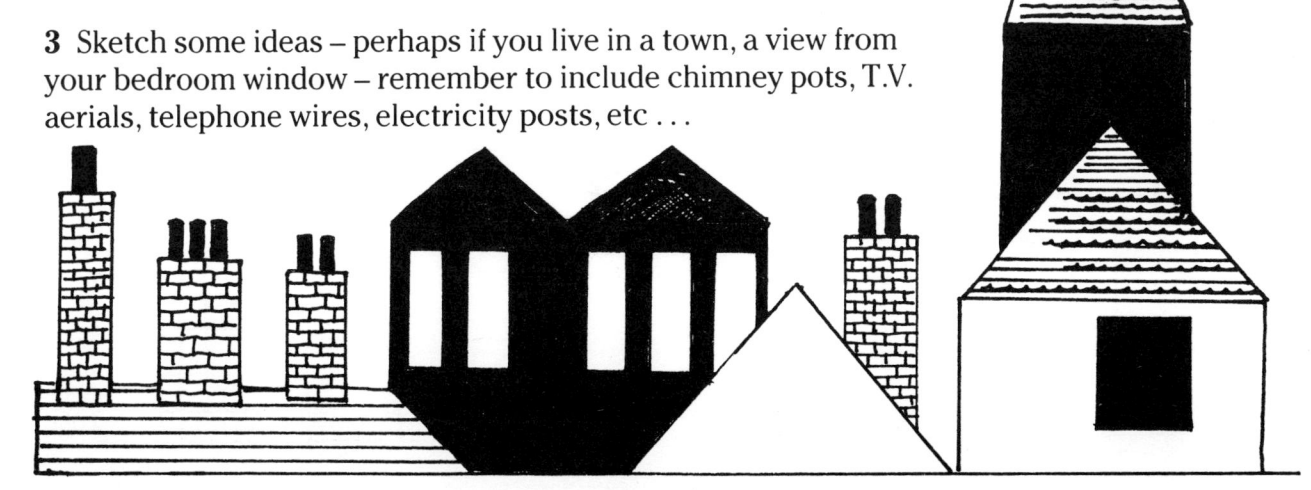

3 Sketch some ideas – perhaps if you live in a town, a view from your bedroom window – remember to include chimney pots, T.V. aerials, telephone wires, electricity posts, etc . . .

4 Using the silhouetted buildings as an idea, simplify the shapes into triangles, rectangles and squares. Use the drawing as a template. Cut out each individual shape from the paper, and cover with fabric in the usual patchwork way.

5 It is very important that the shapes are kept simple and few in number. When the patchwork shapes are completed, sew them together to resemble the original design. Remove the tacking stitches and the paper if you wish, and press before sewing it onto your tie-dye or batik background.

6 Finer detail, for example, TV aerials, chimney pots, telephone wires, smoke, can be added later using hand sewn stitches. Smoke can also be added using teased-out wadding which can be glued on. The amount of finish given to the project depends on your imagination, ability and available time.

Project 2 Life in the garden – floor cushion for a child

Points to consider before starting the project:

>Where will the floor cushion be used?
>Will it receive much rough handling?
>Will it need to be washed frequently?

Suggested uses:

>a child's bedroom
>a nursery/playgroup
>a children's ward in hospital
>in the garden
>a comfort toy for a maladjusted child

Draw up a design brief considering the following:

>available fabrics
>suitability of fabrics
>colour, size, cost
>equipment available
>production of template and/or pattern and design

Suggested size: 100 cm × 100 cm

Suggested fabric:

>the fabric will relate to the end use of the cushion; fabric colour will be important.

Working hints

1 Collect pictures from nature books of butterflies, insects and flowers.

2 Sketch ideas on paper, simplifying the shapes so that they can be adapted into patchwork forms.

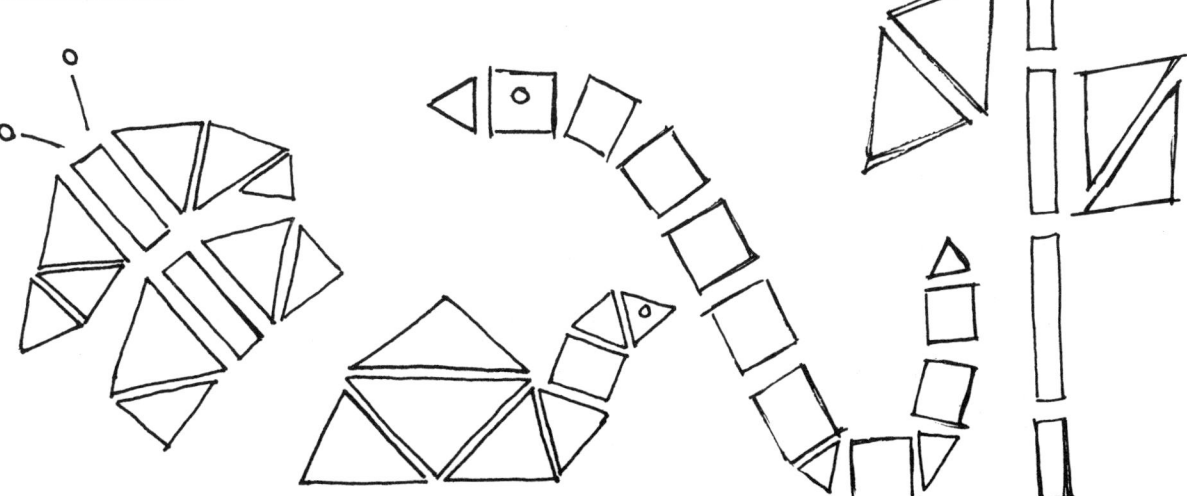

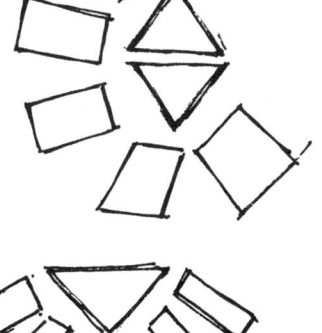

3 Create your design, placing the shapes in an interesting way. It is important to consider the size of the finished drawing at this point, because these shapes, drawn on your paper, will be the templates for the completed patchwork shape.

4 The fabric used for the patchwork shapes should be colourful to attract a child's attention, but be sufficiently simple in design so as not to confuse, or detract from the intended image.

5 Cut out each individual shape from the paper and cover with fabric (see page 19).

6 Sew these individual shapes together to complete the garden life design. Position them, then sew them onto the background.

7 This cushion must be strong enough to withstand handling by children.

8 The back of the cushion may have:

> a plain fabric of suitable strength, colour and quality
> a repeat of first side
> a different design, created by you

Project 3 Patchwork oven gloves

Points to consider before starting the project:
Because these gloves will be used to handle hot dishes, the following considerations must be made:

> the fabric must be hard-wearing
> the wadding must be of sufficient thickness to absorb the heat
> they must be comfortable and safe to wear

Draw up a design brief considering the following:

> the possibility of using up small pieces of scrap fabric, providing it is suitable for the purpose
> colour and cost
> equipment available
> production of template and/or pattern

Suggested size:

> the pattern is made by drawing around your own hand

Suggested fabric:

> scraps of cotton fabric for the patchwork
> 50 cm of plain cotton for the lining
> 50 cm of 110 g polyester wadding
> 85 cm of cotton binding

Working hints

1 Make the pattern by resting your hand (fingers together) on a sheet of newspaper and drawing around it. Then add 3 cm all round for the seams.

2 Cut out your paper pattern.

3 Fold cotton lining fabric in half and cut out the glove pattern twice.

4 Cut four glove pieces from the wadding.

5 Make a piece of patchwork that measures approximately 90 cm × 35 cm. Stick to a simple template shape and do not make the shapes too small.

6 Cut out the glove pattern in doubled fabric as you did for the lining.

7 Open out the lining pieces so that you have two left hand pieces and two right hand pieces.

8 Tack the wadding to each piece of lining.

9 Stitch together in pairs of left and right with unpadded sides together, taking 15 mm seams.

10 Trim wadding from the seam allowance.

11 Clip round the curves and inside the thumb.

12 With right sides together, stitch each pair of patchwork pieces together taking 10 mm seams.

13 Clip round the curves and turn to the right side.

14 Slip wadded lining into the patchwork gloves, wrong sides together and tack the wrist edges together.

15 Fold the cotton binding over the raw edges and stitch in place.

16 Loops for hanging the gloves can be made from the remaining binding.

Questions

1 What are the three most important factors for a successful piece of patchwork?

2 Which of the following fabrics are not suitable for patchwork:

    nylon, gingham, jersey, velvet, terylene, printed cotton, hessian, coarse linen, silk, crimplene?

Give reasons why.

3 Draw up a design brief to show how the patchwork shapes could be used for a border design on a quilt:

        rectangles with triangles
        squares with triangles
        stars made from diamonds

Tasks for further study

1 Patchwork has a very interesting history. Give a detailed account of its development.

2 In this chapter only a few kinds of patchwork shapes have been mentioned. Find out about some of the other more complicated shapes which can be used. Draw diagrams to illustrate your answer.

Chapter 3
Soft Sculpture

When fabric is modelled it becomes sculptural – a form in space. Three-dimensional forms, simply made up in fabric, can be interesting and attractive. Padded, stuffed three-dimensional objects, serving no particular function, can be developed into fascinating art forms and can be entertaining and ornamental.

The impression of volume and relief can be given by quilting, padded patchwork and covered card shapes. Geometric three-dimensional forms are the simplest to make, e.g. balls and spheres. The construction of irregular forms requires more planning and care when making-up. It is usually advisable to make each section of the form individually, adding all necessary decoration to the flat surface before making up the three-dimensional form.

Cotton wool can be used to stuff the small shapes. Wadding, kapok or foam rubber chips is suitable for most of the sculptures suggested in the projects, with cut up tights or rags for large forms.

Equipment

- templates and patterns – some are included in this chapter

A range of the following would be useful:

- a wide selection of scrap fabric, trimmings, braids, lace and button moulds, small quantities of felt in strong colours e.g. red, green, brown, maroon, yellow and orange
- embroidery cottons and sewing threads in a range of colours and thicknesses
- card, glue and scissors
- stuffing, e.g. cotton wool, kapok and foam chips

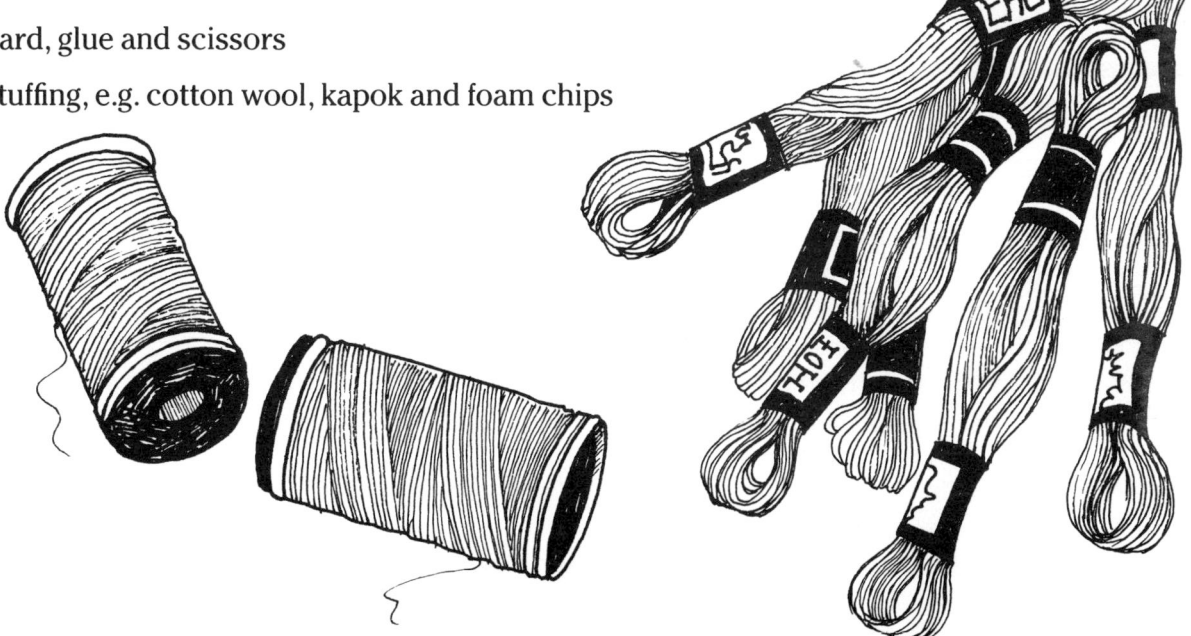

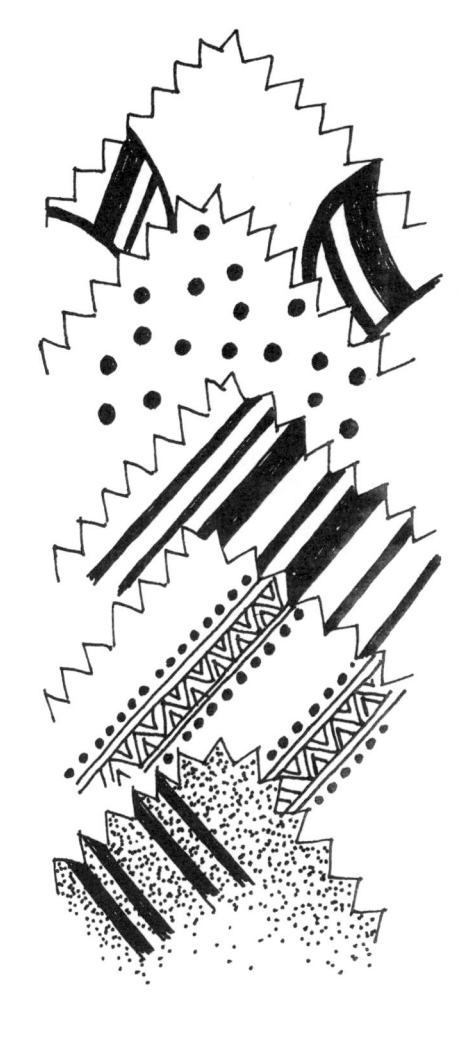

Record keeping

Make a clear presentation of all the stages of your work in your note-book or folder.

To achieve this – things to consider:

1 After any exploration work, or experiments, always note down exactly what you did and record your results.

2 List the main points to consider when making soft sculptures – suitable fabrics, basic construction processes, and effect of suitable construction and finish.

3 List the many uses of soft sculpture items. If you made a soft toy, consider the safety and educational needs and the role of toys in the development of manipulative skills in children.

4 Show how you developed your original designs for your project.

5 When you evaluate your project, remember to include an estimation of cost and amount of fabric used.

Exploring soft sculpture

Constructing and making up of three-dimensional forms must be well planned, so it is advisable always to begin with simple shapes.

The patterns must be accurately drafted and constant investigation and experimentation is essential to discover the potential of all fabrics.

Choice of fabrics

There are some fabrics which work in soft sculpture and suit the purpose. There are others which work but are impracticable, and some which will not work at all. In making your choice, always ask yourself the following questions in relation to your project:

>Does colour need to be an important consideration?
>Does the fabric need to be tough?
>Will the fabric fray?
>Will texture need to be considered?
>Will the fabric stretch?
>Will it withstand frequent washing?
>Does it need to be absorbent?

With these points in mind keep a record in your folder of the following:

1 Collect samples of the following fabrics and sort them into 'suitable', 'impracticable' and 'unsuitable' categories.

Felt, cotton, poplin, hessian, canvas, cotton towelling, jersey, nylon, velvet, satin, printed cotton, denim.

2 Take a small sample of fabric and practise the stitches you will use in your sculpture e.g. French knots and satin stitch. Try graduating the tones in your satin stitch sample, e.g. a yellow, orange, red graduation.

3 Explore next, the possibilities of using two of the fabrics – felt and hessian – for a soft sculpture form. Use the template of the strawberry (page 34), follow the instructions carefully and make two samples of the fruit, one in felt and one in hessian. Which is the most successful fabric for the three dimensional form? Why?

Any embroidery should be done before cutting out. Texture can be added by using embroidery stitches. French knots for pips on strawberries, satin stitch for the effect of light, the colour of the thread indicating shadows and highlights.

Simple experiments

Make a record of what you did for your folder.

1 Take a piece of striped cotton approximately 25cm square, a large handful of stuffing and some small rubber bands. Use a piece of the stuffing (about the size of a small apple) and lay it onto the fabric on the wrong side. Lift it up into the fabric tying the neck tightly with either a rubber band or piece of thread to hold the bundle in place. Use up the rest of the stuffing to make little bumps all over the surface of the fabric. The striped cotton takes on interesting three-dimensional forms, and the fabric between becomes pleated and gathered. Draw the sample.

2 Using the template for the orange (page 38) make two small balls, one in felt and one in cotton towelling. Which is the most suitable toy for a young baby? Give reasons.

3 Button moulds are easy to use if you follow the manufacturer's directions. Fine fabrics may need several thicknesses to cover well and it may help to wet the fabric first. Try to use a variety of sizes of button mould.

These shapes are suitable for grapes, cherries and berries. Draw a design to show how they could be used as an addition to an appliqued picture.

4 Wash a small sample of each of the following fabrics in detergent and hot water. Record your results.

      printed cotton, hessian, nylon, felt, pure woollen fabric

Relate your results to the suitability of using the fabric for three-dimensional sculpture.

5 Trapunto quilting is sometimes known as padded quilting. Two thicknesses of fabric are used, and the areas of the design which are enclosed with stitching are filled with padding from the underside. Follow the diagrams carefully, and do a small sample.

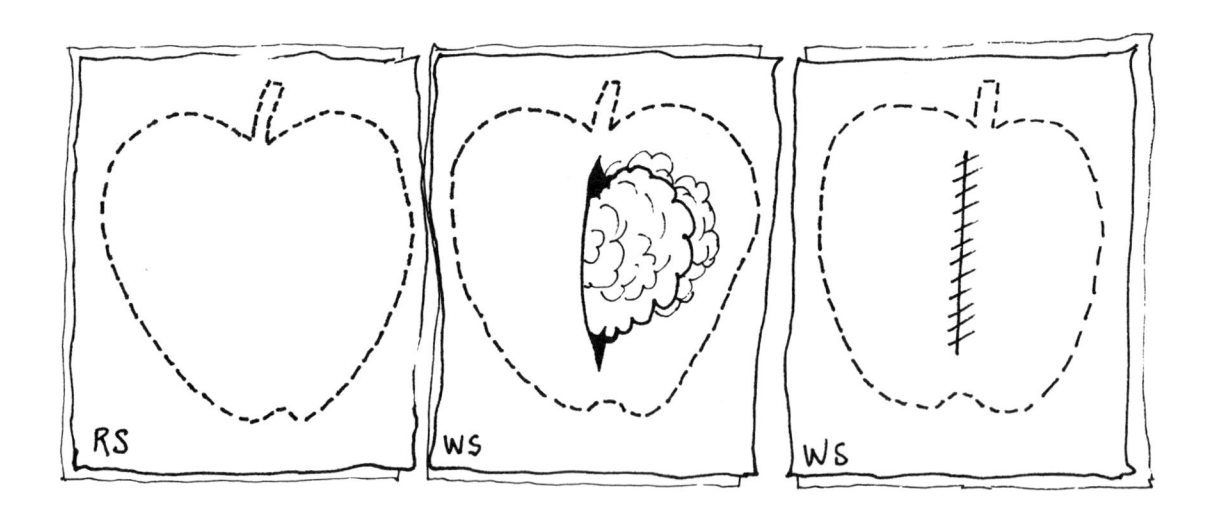

1 Outline the shape in stitching on the right side of the fabric. On the wrong side, make a small slit in the backing fabric.

2 Stuff with kapok or wadding.

3 Oversew the slit.

Project ideas – food in soft sculpture

Before starting any of the following projects it would be useful to do the following:

1 Collect pictures or examples of different kinds of food and drink.

2 Select one item with interesting texture, colour and shape, e.g. black forest gateaux, strawberries and cream. Patterns are included in this chapter for different items of food. These ideas may be used for other designs.

3 On paper, draw and colour in your idea, not forgetting to keep a record in your folder.

4 You are now ready to transfer your idea into fabric. At this stage you must understand measurement so as to measure accurately, and appreciate the limitations of fabrics.

Points to consider before starting each of the projects in this section.

Which of the items are you going to make?

1 A purely decorative three-dimensional object to display in a room
2 Some small three-dimensional shapes that are to be part of a collage or appliqued picture
3 A mobile to hang in a child's bedroom
4 A soft toy for a toddler

Draw up a design brief considering the following:

- will the fabric need to be washable?

- must it be light e.g. if it is for a mobile?

- will the fabric mix with others in the project?

- will it collect dust, will this be a problem?

- could the items be made from available scrap fabric or do you want to buy new fabric and pay more?

Suggested size:

templates and measurements are provided for each project

Suggested fabric:

There is a list of equipment on page 29. The fabric used depends entirely upon the end use of the item.

Project 1 Strawberries
– pincushions, decoration for gateaux or mobiles

Materials – scraps of red and green felt, yellow embroidery thread, stuffing and a small twig.

Working hints

1 Trace the pattern for your strawberry.

2 Cut it out and pin to the red felt.

3 Cut out the red felt shape.

4 Using yellow embroidery threads and French knots, work on the seeds as the diagram shows.

5 Fold the felt in half, right side inside.

6 Join the seam as shown in the diagram.

7 Turn the right side out and run a strong gathering thread around the top edge.

8 Stuff the strawberry, then pull up the gathers tightly and fasten off.

9 Collect a small dry twig for the stalk.

10 Use green felt to cut an irregular star shape for the top.

11 Stick one end of the twig through the centre hole of the green felt, and push the twig into the top of the strawberry.

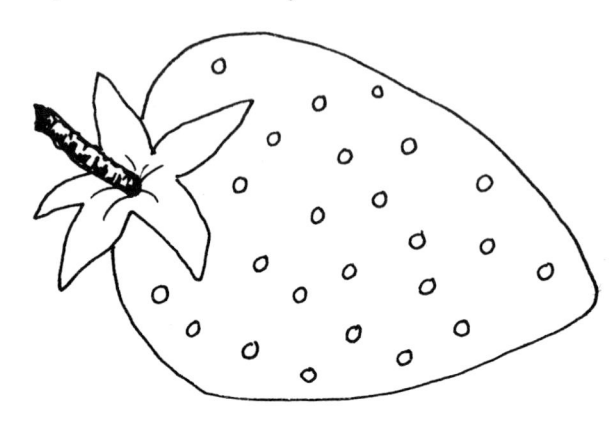

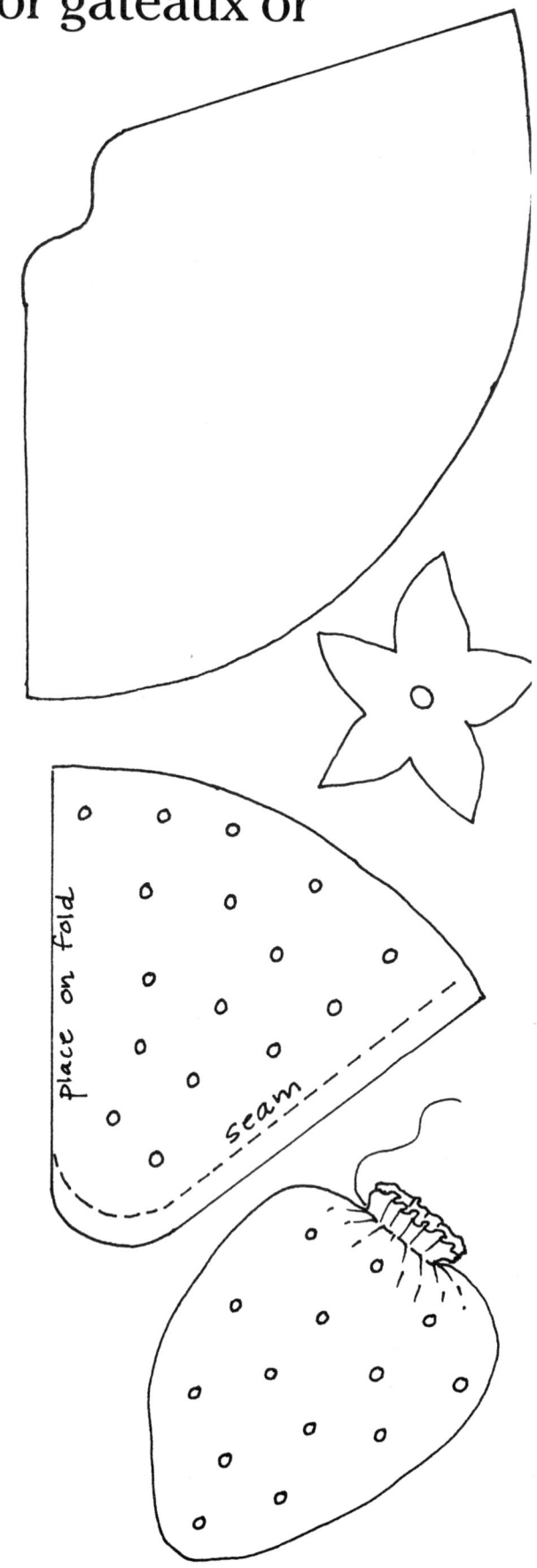

Project 2 Cherries
– decoration for gateaux or appliqued picture

Materials – scraps of red, brown or maroon felt, stuffing.

Working hints

1 Trace the pattern.

2 Cut it out and pin it to the felt.

3 Cut out the felt shape.

4 Run a strong gathering thread around the outside of the shape.

5 Stuff, then pull up the gathers tightly and fasten off.

This pattern can also be used for grapes or for chocolate buttons which may be used to decorate the gateaux on the following page.

This pattern can also be used for cauliflowers. Make a number of each shape and then join together before adding fabric leaves. You will need to consider which fabrics would be best for the cauliflower and which for the leaves.

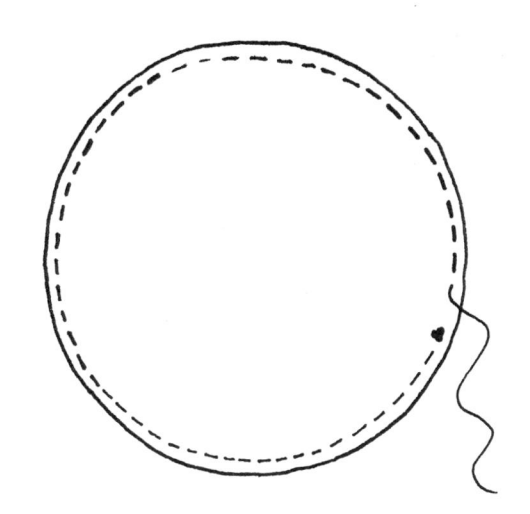

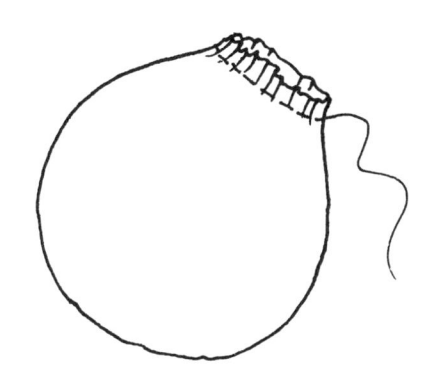

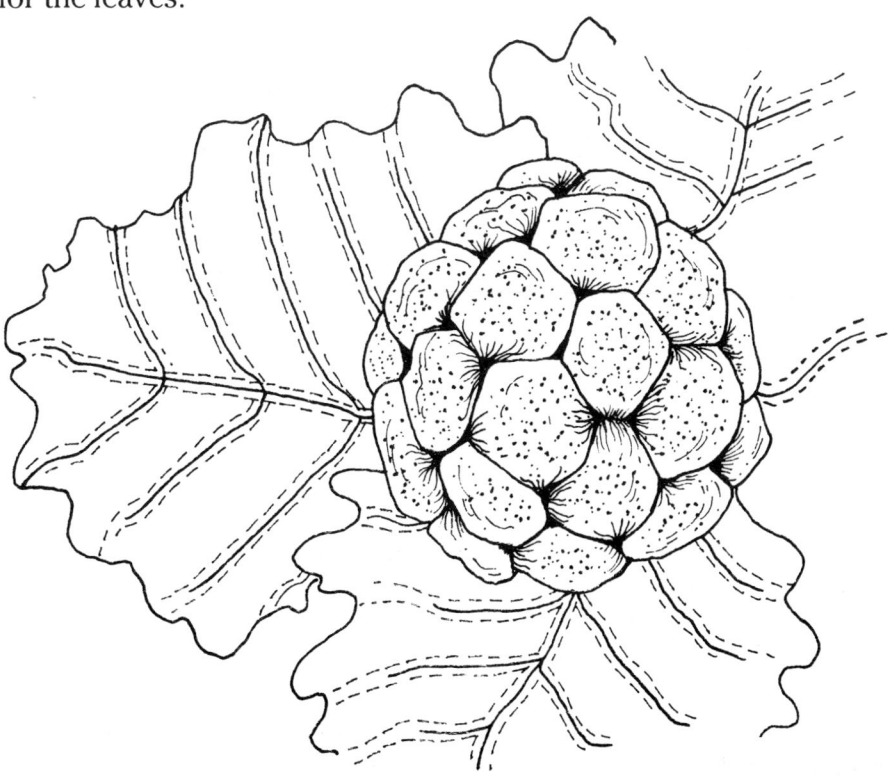

Project 3 Gateaux or birthday cake – a 'fun object' which, enlarged, could be a cushion

Materials – any fabric which would be suitable in colour and texture for a cake, e.g. brown, cream, pink crimplene or cotton, etc. Some scraps of red brown or maroon felt, for cherries or chocolate buttons. You will also need lace and braid for icing, felt for decoration, e.g. numbers and names and coloured pipe cleaners for candles.

Working hints

1 Cut two circles of fabric of a suitable colour, weight and texture, each ten inches in diameter.

2 Cut one strip thirty two inches long and four inches wide.

3 Decide how the cake is to be decorated, e.g. a birthday cake decorated with appliqued numbers, names or motifs, or decorated as a gateaux with fruit, chocolate buttons and lace for icing.

4 Decorate one circle accordingly.

5 Pin, tack and then sew the long strip around the decorated circle, keeping the right side, inside.

6 Sew the second circle onto the strip, which is the base of the cake, leaving a small gap so that the cake can be turned right-side out, and then stuffed.

7 Sew up the gap.

8 Coloured pipe cleaners can be pushed into the top circle to simulate candles.

Project 4 A bunch of bananas
– soft toys, ornamental art forms

Materials – yellow felt, stuffing.

Working hints

1 Draw up a pattern from the graph. For a bunch of 5 bananas, cut ten side pieces on the straight of the grain from 50 cm of yellow felt.

2 Cut 5 each of the back and front pieces, all on the bias.

3 Decorate the felt pieces with simple hand-sewn stitches to show blemishes or brown dots on the skin.

4 Make each banana separately by stitching the pieces together, right side inside. It may be easier to clip up the seam allowance (1 cm) before sewing the pieces together, then it will be easier to ease the curves of the side piece in place.

5 Leave 5 cm open at the stalk end of one seam on each banana.

6 Trim the seams.

7 Turn the bananas right side out and stuff with wadding. Slipstitch the openings and stuff the stalks.

8 Sew the bananas together carefully to form a bunch.

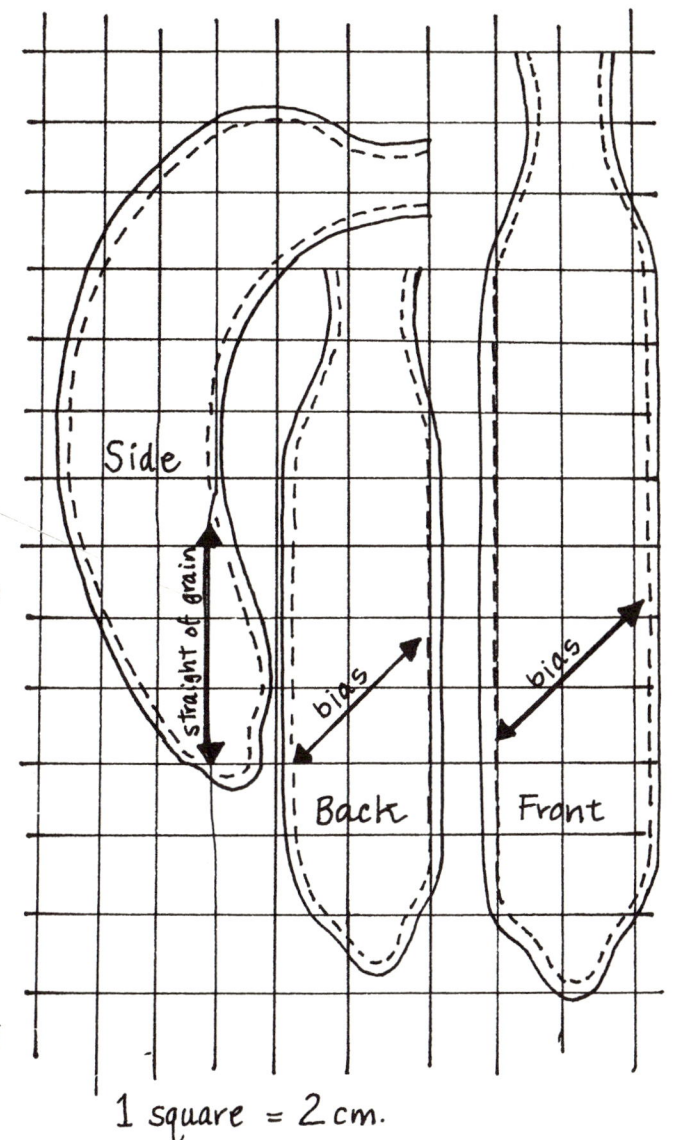

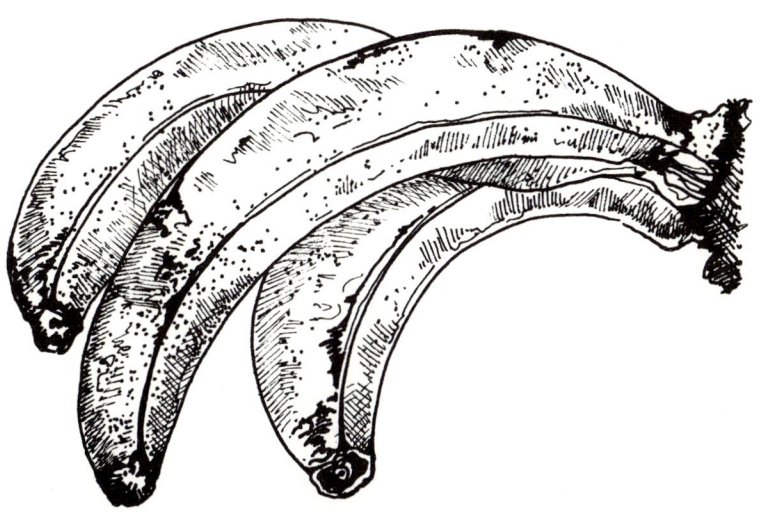

Project 5 Oranges and apples
– soft toys and small decorative objects

Materials – orange, red, green and white felt. Stuffing, card, glue and embroidery threads.

Working hints

1 To make a whole orange or apple, trace the pattern pieces.

2 Cut out shape number 1 eight times, using either the orange, red or green felt.

3 Sew together the eight pieces from the wrong side, leaving a small gap in one of the seams.

4 Turn to the right side, stuff and sew up the opening.

5 At this stage, texture can be added to the three-dimensional shape by using French knots or satin stitch, which will give the surface of the fruit interest and colour.

6 A stalk can be made for the apple by rolling a small piece of brown felt around a twig, glueing in place, and then inserting it into the top of the apple.

Working hints to make half an orange or apple

1 Cut out shape number 2 eight times, using either orange, red or green felt.

2 Sew together from the wrong side and stuff.

3 Cut out shape number 3 from card, and then cut a circle from the white felt, three centimetres larger than the diameter of the card.

4 At this stage, detail can be embroidered onto the circle of white felt.

5 Stick the white felt circle onto the card circle. Before placing on the orange or apple base snip the white card overlap (see diagram) and glue.

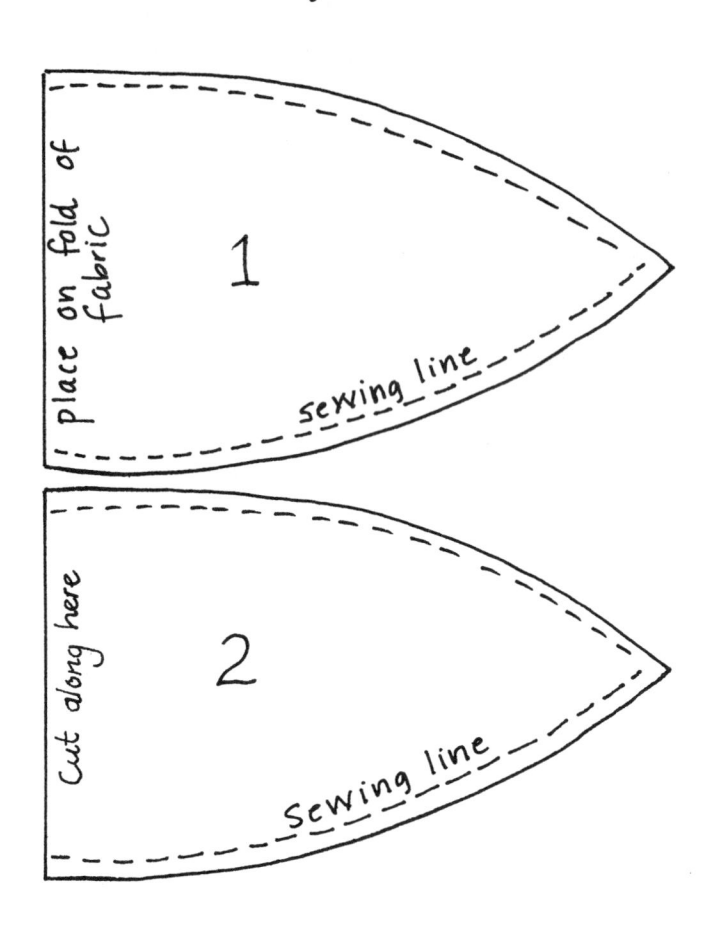

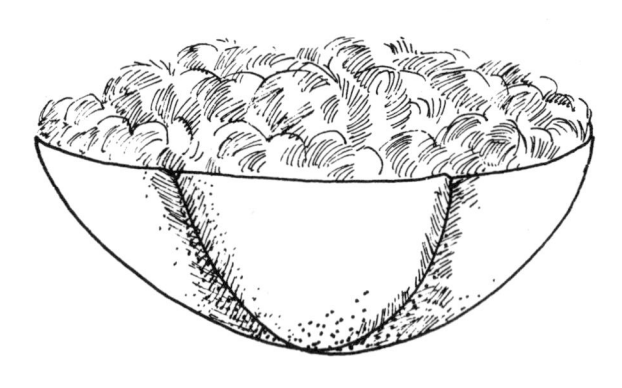

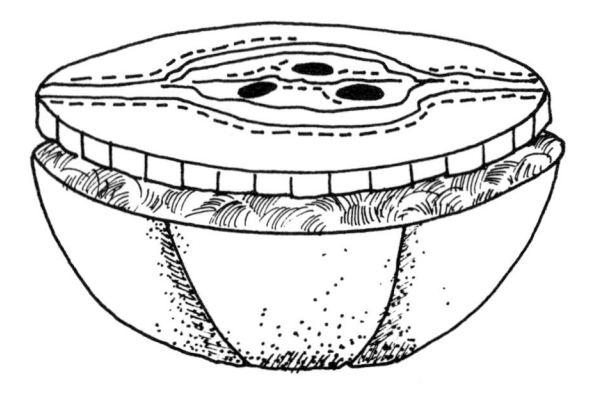

Project 6 A hamburger
– 3-D decorative object, pin cushion

The pattern for the apples and oranges can also be adapted to make a hamburger.

Working hints

1 Using the pattern for the half orange or apple, cut out sixteen pieces of pattern number 2 (eight for each half), using brown felt.

2 Sew the pieces together in the same way as for the half orange or apple.

3 When stuffing the base, only add a small amount of stuffing so as to keep the shape fairly flat.

4 Assemble and make in exactly the same way as the halves of fruit.

5 Simple cut out shapes of green felt to represent lettuce leaves, red felt for tomatoes, can be glued in place between the hamburger halves making sure they are visible.

It is possible to use these patterns indefinitely, adapting them to alter scale and purpose.

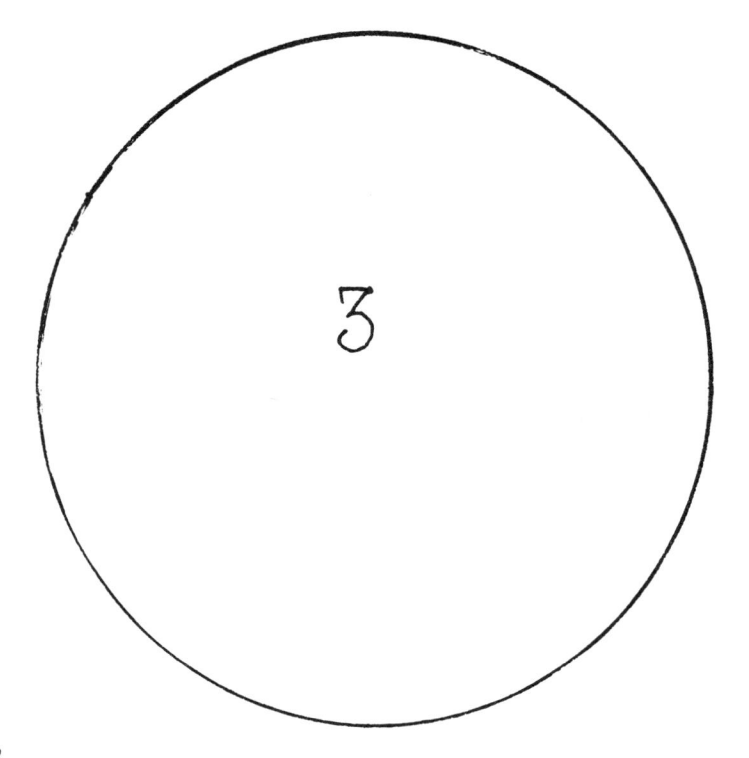

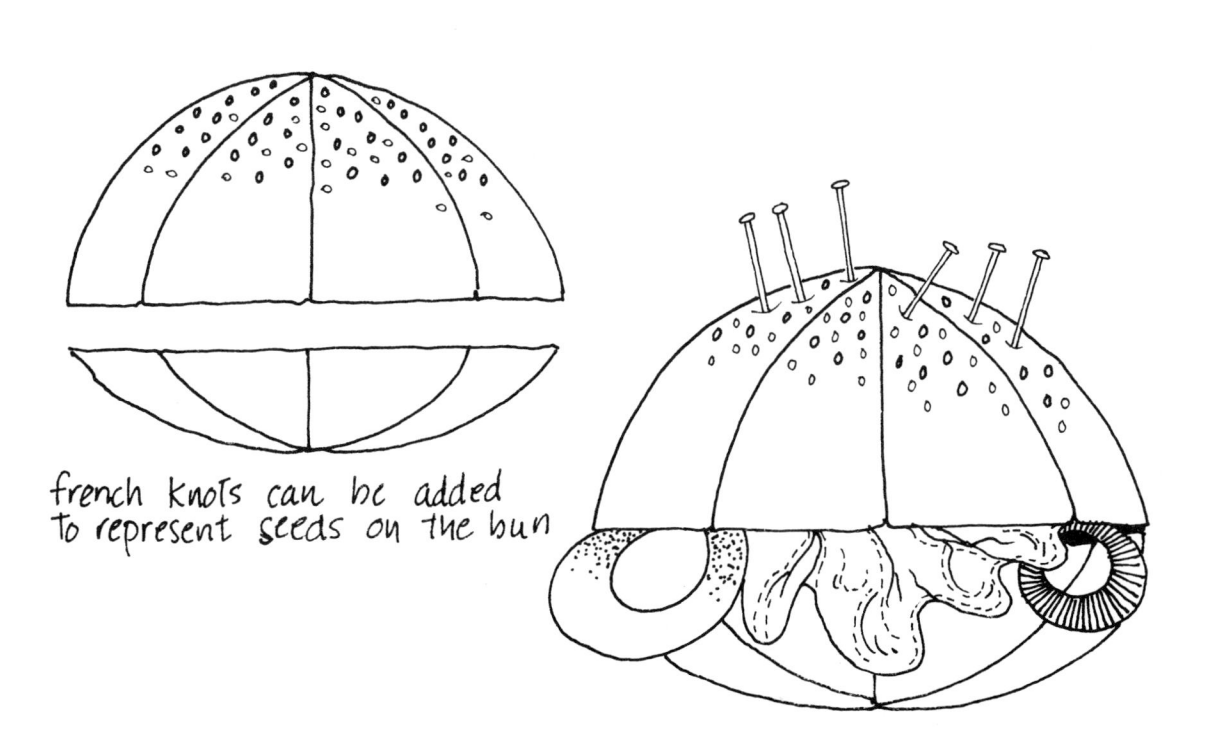

french knots can be added to represent seeds on the bun

Questions

1 List the ways in which fabric can be modelled to make it look three dimensional.

2 Design an appliqued picture in which at least two techniques are used to show how fabric can be modelled in a three-dimensional way.

3 Give 3 reasons why old towels and face cloths are an ideal choice when choosing fabric for soft toys.

4 Some of the patterns in this chapter could easily be adapted to create other items of food, the half orange pattern could be adapted as a mushroom, for example. Some changes would need to be made. Describe in detail, and with the aid of diagrams, how you would adapt the original pattern to make something of your own choice.

5 Cotton towelling is a suitable fabric for soft sculpture forms. Make a list of its properties and suggest two three-dimensional items which could be made from the fabric. Give reasons for your choice.

Tasks for further study

1 Write out a design brief for a life-size soft sculpture of a child that you know.

Work out the cost of the following considerations:

suitable fabric for body
stuffing
clothing
hair
accessories

2 Claes Oldenburg, the American artist made a whole series of soft sculptures using vinyl and other materials, and loosely filled them with kapok. Find out more about the artist and his work.

3 Many of the items in this chapter could be made into soft toys for the family to help human development. How do toys help in the development of manipulative skills? How would the needs of a handicapped child differ?

Chapter 4
Texture

The qualities of texture can be appreciated both by sight and by touch. Any texture is enhanced by contrast. By selecting and using materials that have different surface qualities a design will become more interesting to look at. The shine on satin, the pile on velour and velvet rely on light and shadow to improve their appearance.

The surface of a fabric may be interesting enough to create a textural design, but there are lots of ways in which texture can be added. All designs can be enhanced by the addition of appropriate hand-sewn stitches, beads, braids, sequins, buttons etc. There are also many techniques in textiles for creating texture.

As fabrics and threads are rich in contrasting textures, different combinations should be tried out and assessed.

Careful planning is essential to choose the most suitable techniques for the purpose.

Equipment
A selection of the following would be useful.

- waste materials—plastic mesh onion/fruit bags
- fur, leather, suede off-cuts
- old washed tights or clothes
- decorative ribbon, cords and braids
- knitting and rug wools
- thick, thin and metallic threads and string
- beads, sequins, buttons
- scraps of felt
- background fabric for example hessian or calico
- wadding or thin foam
- paper, card, pencils and glue

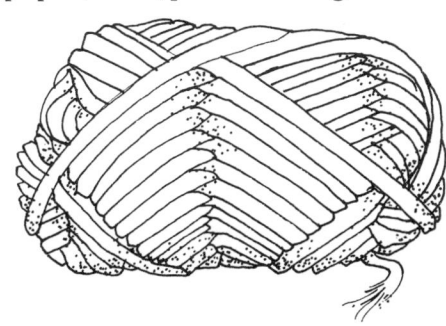

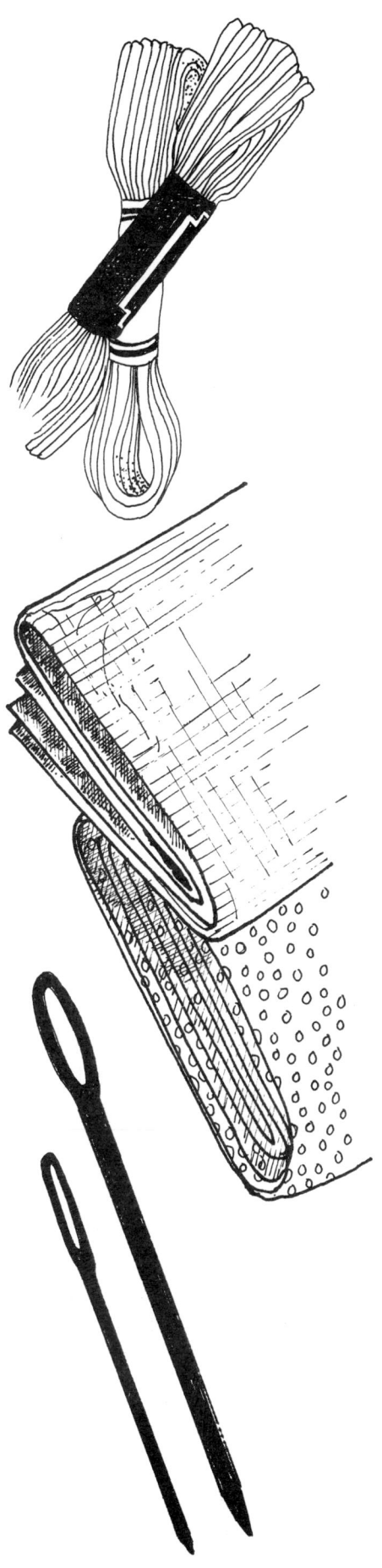

Record keeping

Make a clear presentation of all the stages of your work in your note-book or folder.

To achieve this – things to consider:

1 After any exploration work, or experiments, always note down exactly what you did and record your results.

2 Make a list and include samples of fabric which have a textural quality.

3 Note down ways in which texture can be created.

4 Show how you developed your original designs for your project.

5 When you evaluate your project, remember to include an estimation of cost and amount of fabric used.

Exploring texture

There are many ways in which texture can be created in textiles. Some of the techniques are simple but others need more skill. As the range of textures it is possible to achieve is very wide it is important to plan ahead and choose the best techniques for each individual project.

Some of the many techniques that will create texture are:

hand-sewn stitches	smocking
machine embroidery	fraying
quilting	padding
drawn fabric	prodding
plaiting	couching

Adding beads, braids and sequins.

1 First, select from a box of fabric scraps those whose texture you feel could be useful in a collage. Close your eyes, then test with your fingertips before commenting on the surface of the fabrics.

- Examine how some of the fabrics feel and look – are they soft, shiny, coarse, rough, smooth or chunky?
- When looking at and touching fabrics we become aware that the surface texture can compare to things seen.

2 From your collection of fabrics select which you think is the equivalent texture for the following:

tree bark, clouds, ploughed fields, paved paths, stone walls, your pet.

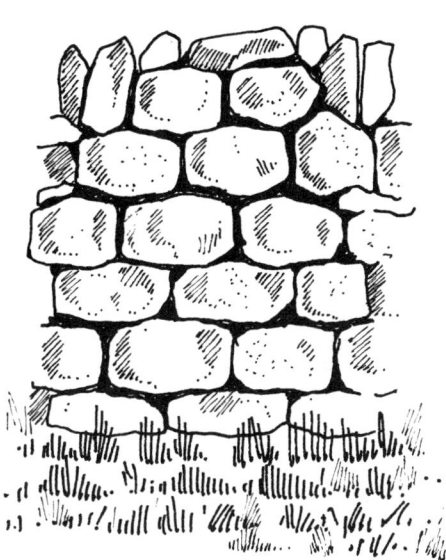

3 It would be impossible in this chapter to describe in detail all the techniques listed. There are many books available that specialise in teaching the skills. However, with the additional help available from a book, attempt the following; not forgetting to keep a sample for your folder.

- drawn fabric – warp and weft threads are pulled and distorted to form holes in the fabrics and patterns on the surface of the fabric.

- couching – threads and yarns are laid on the surface of the fabric and held in position with stitches worked over them.

- hand-sewn stitches – use various background fabrics, change the scale, use thick and thin yarn.

- quilting – the otherwise flat surface of the fabric is transformed into an undulating surface (see Trapunto quilting page 32).

- smocking – this is a technique used to control fullness. By using a few simple smocking stitches, the technique can be used to represent:

    movement in water
    the bark of a tree
    undulating landscape.

However, it is the ability to adapt these techniques into a creative and original design that is important. The projects in this chapter attempt to do just that.

43

Simple experiments

Make a note of what you did for your folder.

1 Using one colour of fabric, but making use of a variety of tones and textures, create a simple design based on different sized squares and rectangles. Arrange the cut-out fabric shapes before sticking them down with glue onto thin card. Glue is a quick method of working for simple experiments.

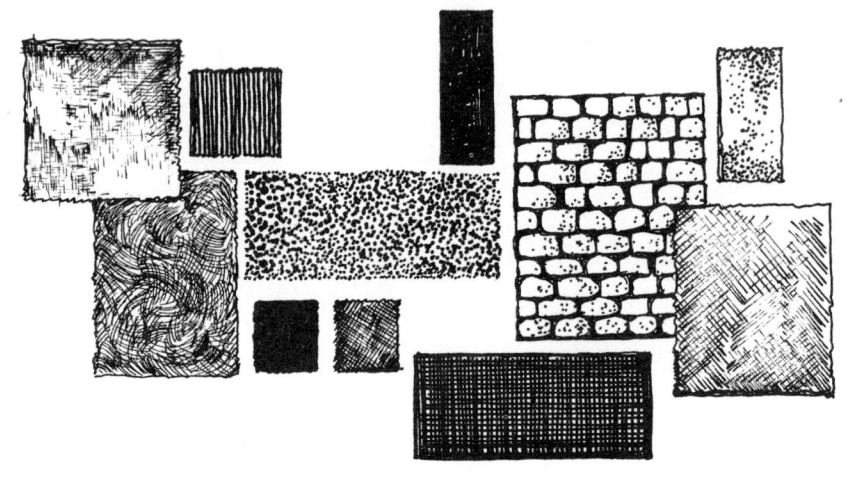

2 Find a pebble, stone or piece of rock that has an interesting surface, interpret the surface texture using fabric, yarn, threads, and at least three different embroidery stitches and two techniques.

3 Plait together in approximately 20 cm lengths the following combinations:

>rug wool, ribbon and string
>chenille, raffia and cord
>cut plastic strips, braid and mohair
>some of your own combinations

Couch down your plaited strips onto a hessian background to create a design based on the idea of spirals.

4 Padding is generally one or more layers of felt – each layer underneath the top one is cut slightly smaller than the one above. The layers are tacked together in position then the final layer is stitched down with close together stitches before the shape is covered in fabric.

Experiment with padding using felt, but also do some samples using thin foam, wadding and card. Keep your shape simple.

5 Smocking is a decorative embroidery technique used to control fullness in fabric. Work a small sample, using stem stitch and wave stitch, to represent the bark on a tree trunk. Restrict your colour scheme and try tie-dyeing the fabric first. You may need to refer to a book if this is your first attempt at smocking.

Project 1 The King of Hearts – a cushion

Points to consider before starting the project:

> As it is a cushion with a textured surface it will be more interesting and useful to certain groups of people.
> Could it be functional as well as decorative?
> Will it receive much wear and tear?
> Is it possible to make the cushion out of available bits and pieces, therefore reducing cost?

Suggested uses:

> for an old person to give comfort and support
> for a partially sighted person.

Draw up a design brief considering the following:

> suitability of fabric/yarns/threads
> cost, size, colour
> equipment available
> production of template and/or pattern and design

Suggested size: 42 cm × 32 cm

Suggested fabric:

> calico for the lining
> kapok for the stuffing
> natural or self-coloured fabric for the background
> wools, yarns, beads, sequins, buttons, ribbons

Working hints

The emphasis in this project is texture. Try to vary the techniques as much as possible to make the textural surface of the cushion interesting and pleasing to the touch.

1 Use the King of Hearts from a pack of playing cards.

2 You will see that the detail is intricate and the colour range limited. You will need to simplify your design, breaking down the involved areas of pattern into simple shapes.

3 On a piece of drawing paper measuring 42 cm × 32 cm draw a centred rectangle measuring 35 cm × 20 cm. Draw your design in this measured rectangle.

4 Begin by folding your paper in half and drawing a faint line along the fold.

5 Draw your design in the top half of the paper only – keep the shapes simple.

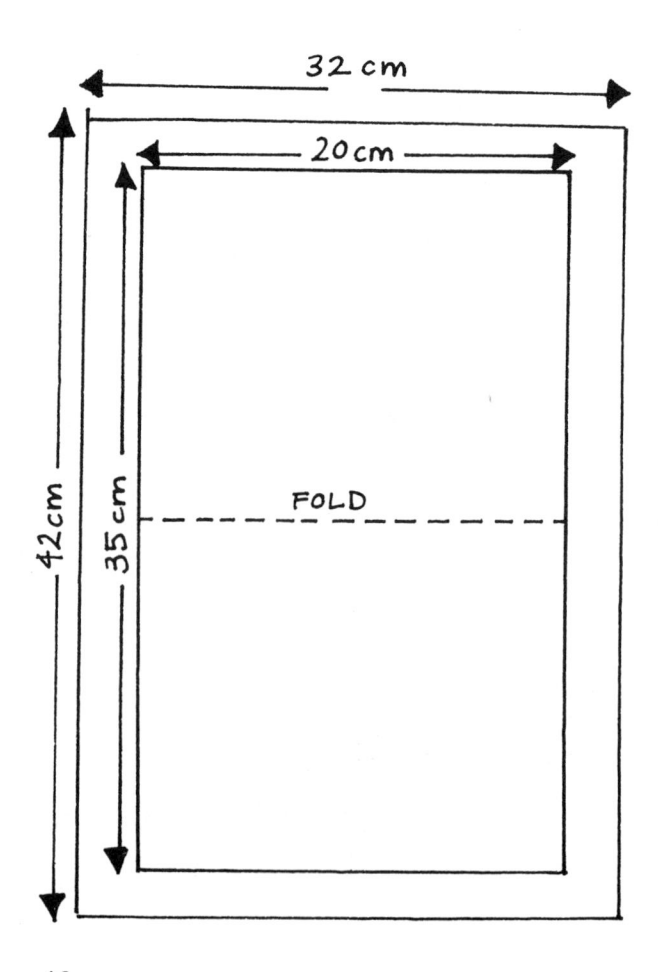

46

6 Trace the design, then place your tracing in reverse for the bottom half of the design (so that the king's head is looking in the opposite direction).

7 Colour in your design.

8 Cut a piece of fabric for the background – see plan for suggested fabrics. The shape should measure 42 cm × 32 cm.

9 Transfer your design onto the background fabric – see diagram.

10 Begin by stitching the face using black embroidery cotton and backstitch.

11 How you fill in the various areas depends on you but you could possibly use some of the following suggestions:

- plaited or couched yarn for the hair
- fur fabric for the ermine
- areas filled in by French knots
- appliqued felt shapes
- woven ribbons and braids for parts of costume
- lace for collars and cuffs.

12 When you have completed your design, cut another piece of fabric the same size for a backing to the cushion. Make up the lining and the cushion, then stuff in the usual way.

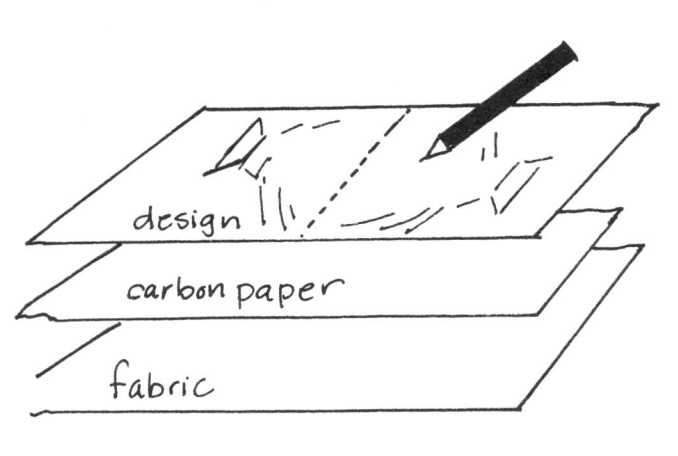

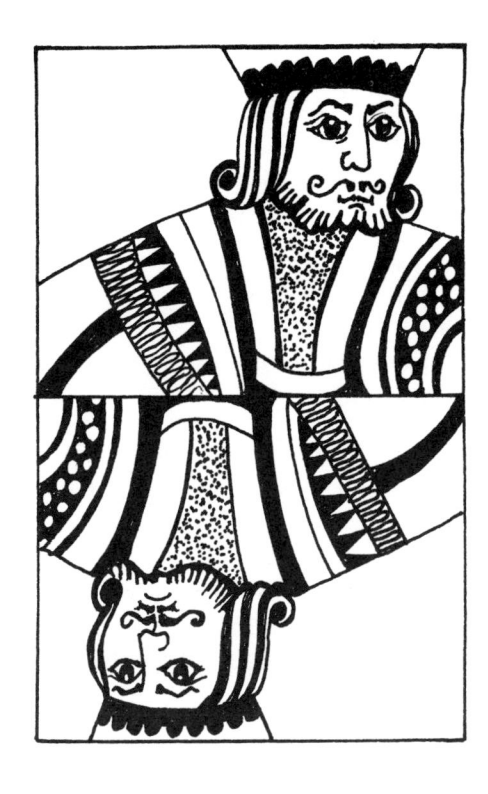

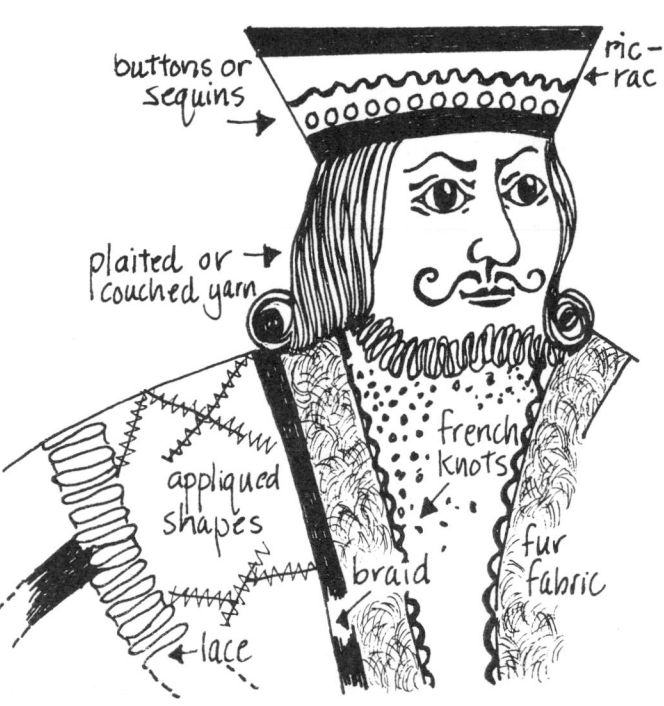

47

Project 2 Aerial views
– a prodded rug using rags

Points to consider before starting the project:

> Will the rug receive much wear?
> As it is a fairly slow technique, have you sufficient time to complete a rug of this size?
> It is cheap to produce – why?
> Could it be decorative as well as functional?

Suggested uses:

> a door mat
> a floor covering for a living room of a country cottage or modern flat
> a wall hanging

Draw up a design brief considering the following:

> size
> suitability of fabric and colour
> equipment available
> production of design, template and/or pattern
> cost

Suggested size:

> 80 cm × 50 cm (this can be easily changed)

Suggested fabric:

> sacking or hessian for the background
> cut or torn coloured rags, in strips about 2 cm wide

Additional equipment:

- for the frame, an old large picture frame 100 cm × 70 cm

OR
- 4 pieces of wooden batten – two 100 cm × 5 cm and – two 79 cm × 5 cm

with
- 4 wing nuts and bolts
- a prodder – a shaped wooden clothes peg – pointed at one end and rounded at the other or a pencil

To make a frame

1 Centre a hole 5 cm in from each end of the four pieces of batten, drill the hole.

2 Assemble the frame using the wing nuts and bolts.

3 Sew the sacking or hessian to the frame, stretching it to make it as tight as possible – see diagram. If you are making a rug to fit a picture frame, stretch and staple the sacking.

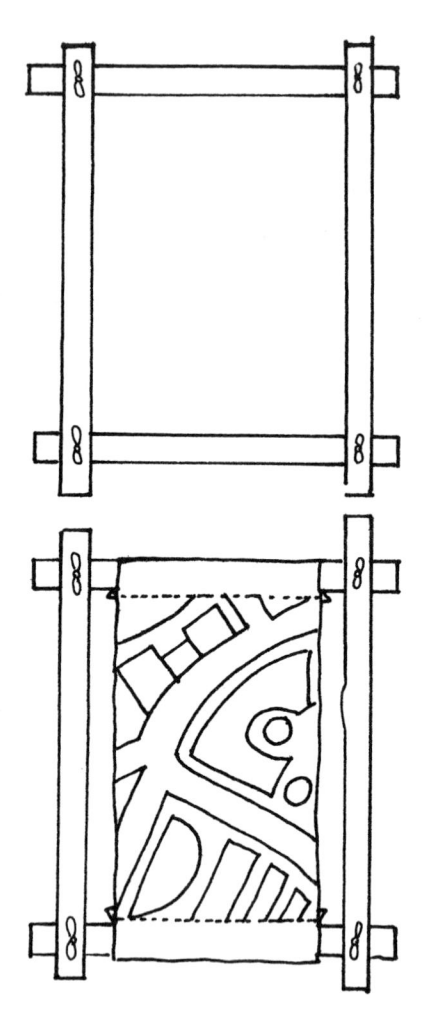

Working hints

1 Begin with a simple design based on aerial photographs of shore lines, land formations, glaciers or cultivated farm land.

2 You could use geography text books for ideas. The illustrations will not only show examples of aerial views but should also show patterns created by railway networks, site location drawings, and maps showing for example distribution of population. These are all interesting ideas to adapt.

3 Use this material for the basis of your design. You will need to simplify the shapes – see diagram.

4 Increase the scale and transfer the idea onto the hessian using a felt-tipped pen.

5 You are now ready to insert the cut rags into the hessian. This technique is called prodding.

6 Hold the frame in front of you, resting it on your lap and against a table.

7 Make a hole in the hessian with a wooden prodder, then take a rag strip and prod a loop through the hole.

8 Remove the prodder and adjust the length of the loop.

9 Work in this way across the hessian filling in the shapes with your chosen coloured rags.

10 The distance between the holes and the lines should be about 2 cm.

11 To start or finish a rag strip leave the strip ends poking out on the right side of the rug.

12 The pile of the rug can be left looped or each loop cut to give a cut pile.

13 When you have completed the rug, remove it from the frame, place it with the looped side down on a table and fold over the unworked hessian or sacking. Either sew it down or glue it.

14 Finally a piece of sacking the same size can be sewn to the back of the rug.

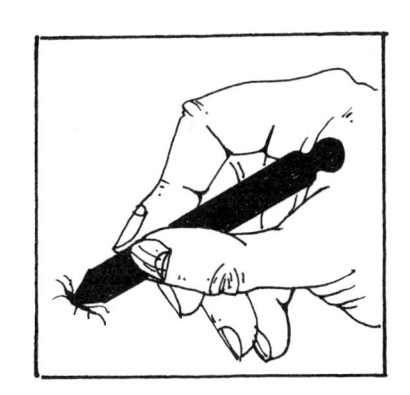

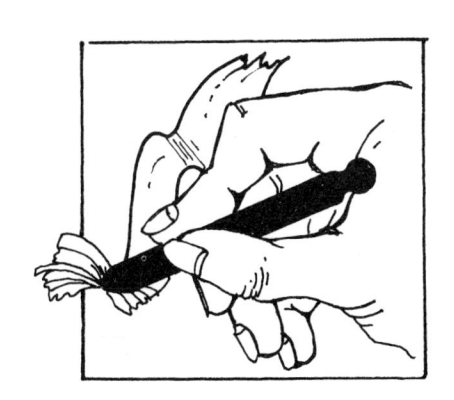

Project 3 Heroes
– a wall hanging

Points to consider before starting the project:

>Where will the wall hanging be used?
>Could it be functional as well as decorative?
>Will it need to be dry cleaned?

Suggested uses:

>A wall hanging or mounted picture for a:
>
>teenager's bedroom
>sixth form common room
>youth centre
>a draft excluder for a small window

Draw up a design brief considering the following:

>production of sketches and finished design
>suitability of fabrics/yarns/threads
>choice and availability of fabrics
>size and colour
>equipment available

Suggested size: 50 cm × 40 cm

Suggested fabric:

>suitable background fabric
>a selection of coloured felt, embroidery cottons, wools
>fabric paints – optional
>calico for the face

Note: When a large amount of felt is used work must be dry cleaned.

twisted cord or wool

plaiting   twisting

couching

50

Working hints

This project allows plenty of scope, both in choice of character and techniques used.

1 Use a large life-size photograph of your hero – a sports personality, pop star, character from a book, film or history.

2 Transfer your photograph onto the calico by using carbon paper.

3 Place the carbon paper in position face downwards on the calico, then put the photograph of your hero on top.

4 Draw over the photograph with a pencil, take care not to allow the fabric and carbon paper to move.

5 Remove the photograph and carbon paper – you should now have an identical image on your calico.

6 Different effects and textures may be achieved by using fabric paint on the face, quilting the nose and chin etc., varying the thickness of the thread used and selecting a variety of embroidery stitches. The hair could be appliqued shapes, couched or plaited wool.

7 Interest can be added with the addition of ear-rings, necklace, buttons and ribbons.

8 Cut the completed face out of the calico and sew it onto a coloured background.

9 Your project is now ready to mount or assemble for a wall hanging.

seeding

running stitch

satin stitch

french knots

Questions

1 Describe the texture of the following fabrics:

   velour, harris tweed, terry towelling, hessian, silk, nylon

2 A fabric with a nap is one with a raised surface. Which fabrics would you put into this category? What qualities would these fabrics have?

3 List the fabrics and techniques that will create texture in any textile project.

4 Terry towelling is a fabric with a looped surface. Why is this fabric used for towels, nappies and sweat bands?

5 Which fabrics would you include under the following headings:

   matt, smooth, fragile, shiny, luxury, loosely-woven

Tasks for further study

1 Describe in detail, and with the aid of diagrams, the difference between English, Italian and Trapunto quilting.

2 Smocking is one method of controlling fullness in fabric. List the other methods and describe each one fully. Include diagrams in your answer.

3 Find out about the variations that can be given to a plain weave to change the texture.

4 For your note book make the following:
  - hand-embroidered sample of french knots in different thicknesses and textures of thread
  - hand-embroidered sample of running stitches and couched stitches of various length and thickness
  - hand-embroidered sample of drawn thread work
  - machine-embroidered sample of Italian and Trapunto quilting

5 A dhurry is a hand made Indian rug. These rugs are cheap, functional and pleasing to look at. The traditional dhurry is usually designed using very simple motifs e.g. stripes, zig-zags, arrowheads etc.
   (a) Visit some shops in your nearest town and see if you can see any of these rugs. Make notes on price, colour and designs used.
   (b) Design your own dhurry using appropriate colours and motifs. Use no more than 5 colours.

Chapter 5
Knitting

During the last ten years, a number of lively designers have taken up knitting and have helped to change the image of a craft once thought dull and boring. The tremendous range of yarns, and the imaginative and creative patterns available, has also helped to popularise the craft.

The first common use of knitting was for stockings and socks when hand-knitting these items provided an extra income for many families. Even now hand-knitting is an important source of income for people, usually women, in the Shetland Islands off the coast of Scotland where beautiful traditional knitting is produced for sale in London and New York and other big cities of the world.

The patterns in hand-knitted garments were often traditional designs for one village or family. For example, in fishing villages the women used to knit their menfolk sweaters with personal designs and sadly it was these patterns which often allowed sailors to identify where a drowned fisherman came from. Even now a Jersey is different to a Guernsey and yet both are islands very close to each other off the coast of France.

The introduction of the knitting machine in 1589, and its subsequent developments, meant that by 1750 there were 14000 machines in use, but women still continued to produce many hand-knitted garments. Today machine knitting is widely used for mass-produced fabrics, but hand knitting is a craft many people practise and great satisfaction can be derived from selecting yarns and patterns.

However, if your skills are limited, great enjoyment and pleasure can still be experienced by producing a sample using only the simplest of stitches. This can be part of a textile project and can be combined with a variety of techniques.

Equipment

- A wide range of yarns – natural and synthetic
- Needles – metal, wood or plastic, in different thicknesses and lengths

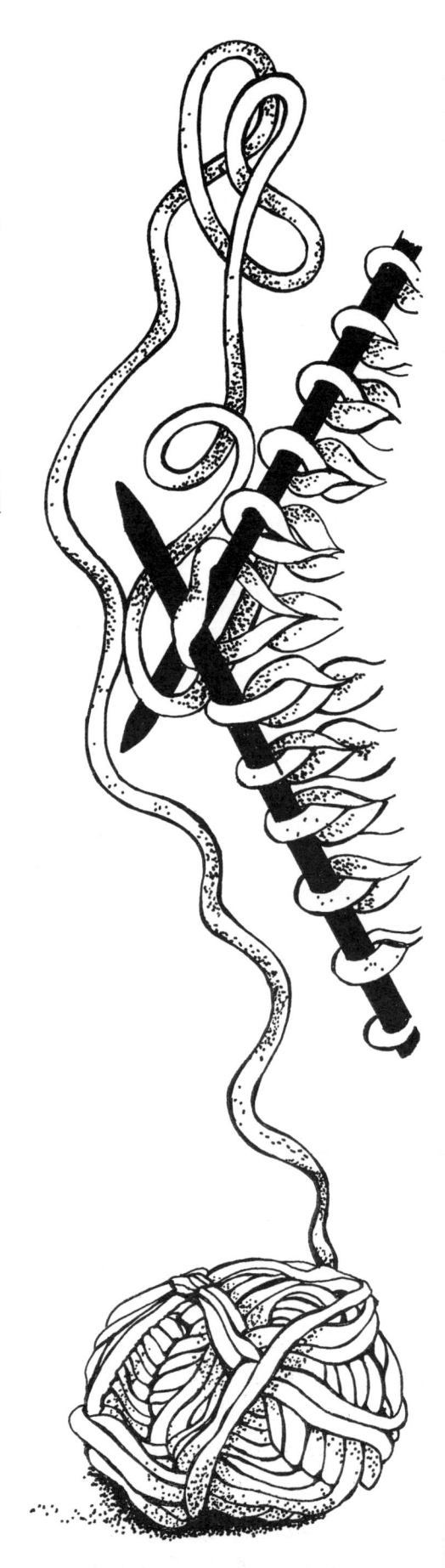

Record keeping

Make a clear presentation of all the stages of your work in your note-book or folder.

To achieve this – things to consider:

1 After any exploration work, or experiments, always note down exactly what you did and record your results.

2 Make a record of the variety of yarns available, their texture, thickness and type.

3 Show how the size of needle can affect the finished product.

4 Knitting is one method of constructing fabric, list the others.

5 Show how the effect of construction can differ by using different stitches, yarns and size of needle.

6 Show how you developed your original designs. If you made a garment and used your project sample as part of the decoration, sketch the outfit and list the processes involved in its construction, estimating costs and amount of fabric used.

7 Evaluate your project.

Exploring hand knitting

Most people assume that knitting is a process whereby exact instructions must be followed in order to complete a wearable garment. In this chapter the projects prove that simple basic knitting stitches can produce samples that can be decorative, imaginative and part of a combination of textile skills.

Types of yarn

The three main sources of fibres from which yarns are made are:

- animals – sheep, camel, llama, angora goat, alpaca, angora rabbit, silk moth
- plants – cotton, flax, wood (used in the manufacture of viscose rayon, acetate and triacetate.)
- synthetic fibres – nylon, polyester and acrylic
  fancy yarns are also available – boucle, chenille, metallic and glitter.

Many of the fibres can be mixed together in different thicknesses, texture and colours.

Collect samples of yarns from each category, stick them into your notebook and label each one.

Thicknesses of yarns

When yarns are made the spun fibres are called plys, which are then twisted together.

- Two-ply, very fine
- Three-ply, fine
- Four-ply, slightly thicker
- Double-knit, quite thick (a large range of yarns come in this thickness)
- Arran, thicker than double knit
- Double double knit, thicker than double knit
- Chunky, very thick
- Icelandic, one of the thickest of all yarns.

What's in a yarn?

Look carefully at a range of yarns. Check for thickness, count the plys, stick samples in your notebook and record your findings.

The label on a ball of yarn gives the following information:

- type of yarn and make
- washing instructions
- where the yarn was made
- weight
- size of needles to use
- colour, shade, dye batch

Take a label from a ball of yarn, stick it in your notebook, record and describe the information/instructions it gives.

Knitting is basically a matter of putting one loop through another and by twisting the loops in various ways different effects can be created.

The loop formation creates a structure that can be distorted by tension. Hand knitting tends to unravel if it is cut so it is best to knit to the required shape.

The basic stitch required for the projects in this chapter is garter stitch and the ability to cast on, increase, decrease and cast off. If you are skilled enough to attempt purl, stocking, ribbing, or moss stitch there is scope for further development.

Explore the possibilities of knitting some small samples using different yarns and thicknesses of needles. Stick the samples into your notebook, beside each sample describe the stitch that you did, the yarn that you chose, and the thickness of the needle. Suggest items of clothing that could be made using the equivalent yarns.

Simple experiments

Make a record of what you did for your folder.

1 Knit a sample 10 cm × 5 cm. Use large needles for this experiment. Before you cast off, slip the loops from the needle. Pull the yarn right across to unravel part of your knitting. (This is easy to do, as hand knitting is an example of weft knitting – each stitch is looped over the one below it.) Assemble this sample in your notebook, then find further examples of weft and warp knitting to stick alongside. List items of clothing that are produced by the two methods.

2 Knit a sample in pure wool, 10 cm × 10 cm. Machine wash at a high temperature. Describe how the sample appears after it has been washed. You could keep the sample for your notebook or folder.

3 Wool can be dyed before spinning or after. Dyeing some wool for yourself can be great fun. Wherever you live you should be able to make your dyes from one of the following sources – lichen, blackberry, tree bark, onions, or iron rust.
   Refer to a book on natural dyeing and try to make at least one sample.

4 Work some knitting on needles of one size then change to needles which are three times larger or smaller. Then try knitting with one needle one size and the other needle a different size.

5 Cut some fabric into thin strips and knit with it – you could even use narrow cotton bandage. Leave the ends to give a shaggy effect. Then try weaving some ribbon, raffia or cord into the knitted sample.

Project 1 Chain mail – a fabric panel or cushion

Consider where the wall hanging or cushion will be used before starting your project.

Suggested uses:

> a fabric panel for: a library, school hall or office
> a cushion for: a caravan, car or lounge/sitting room

Draw up a design brief considering the following:

> available fabrics and yarns
> suitability of fabrics and yarns
> colour, size and cost
> equipment available
> production of design, templates or patterns

Suggested sizes: 70 cm × 70 cm

Suggested fabric:

> hessian for the background
> metallic thread or yarn
> felt, wool, leather scraps
> embroidery threads
> calico and kapok if making the cushion

Working hints

The Bayeux Tapestry is a piece of embroidery produced nine centuries ago. The work is rather like a strip cartoon, each picture telling a different story. The pictures are stitched in two different kinds of woollen thread and in eight different colours, on a long strip of bleached linen.

Using this as the starting point for a project, follow the working hints and adapt the idea taken from the embroidery to create a lively, imaginative design that incorporates a variety of skills.

1 Begin by cutting out your background fabric. Onto this you will arrange the figures, horses, weapons etc. before sticking or sewing them down.

2 The scenes showing the Norman cavalry advancing into battle and the battle scene itself shows the soldiers wearing chain mail. This can be depicted by simple knitting.

3 Using metallic silver coloured yarn or any other suitable thread, knit the shapes illustrated in the approximate sizes.

body 8cm x 5cm
legs 8cm x 3cm
arms 7cm x 3cm

← frayed fabric
← leather and suede off cuts

4 These knitted shapes can be manipulated and distorted before being arranged into the various positions of the soldiers.

5 The horses must be drawn on paper to scale, traced, then the tracing paper cut out acting as the pattern. The fabric for the horses can be any suitable colour and texture – fabrics that fray should not be used.

6 The addition of the leggings, shoes, faces, helmets and large kite-shaped shields around the knitted body shapes will soon give the bodies character and interest.

7 Many features may be added – the more experimentation the better e.g. frayed hessian for the horses manes, thin leather strips or couched wool for the reins, ric rac for borders etc.

8 Sew down the knitted shapes and all other pieces of the design, making sure that they are securely attached.

9 Develop the design into either a fabric panel or a cushion.

Project 2 Cellular structures – garment decoration

Points to consider before starting the project:

Where on a garment is the design to be used?
What style of garment do you envisage using the decoration on?
Will the garment receive rough handling and hard wear?

Suggested uses:

decoration for disco, party, evening wear tops (see page 61)
a framed picture

Draw up a design brief considering the following:

style of garment
purpose of garment
washing/cleaning requirements
fabric – the decoration will be mixed with colour, cost
ability to apply the decoration to a completed garment
production of designs

Suggested size:

the knitted design approx. 16 cm × 12 cm
the complete assembled design is approx. 220 cm × 30 cm
the sizes can easily be reduced; there is no problem in changing the scale.

Suggested fabric and equipment:

fine white cotton for the background 25 cm × 25 cm
Dylon cold water dye
batik pot and wax – optional
one ball of metallic thread, any colour (a suitable type is Twilleys washable goldfingering)
one pair of 10 mm needles
embroidery ring
small beads, sequins, embroidery cottons

Working hints

1 Using a microscope, sketch and draw from slides that show the cross sections of the tissue in stems, roots and leaves. If a microscope is not available many biology and botany books have diagrams that could be used instead.

The drawings that you produce will act as a ready source of reference.

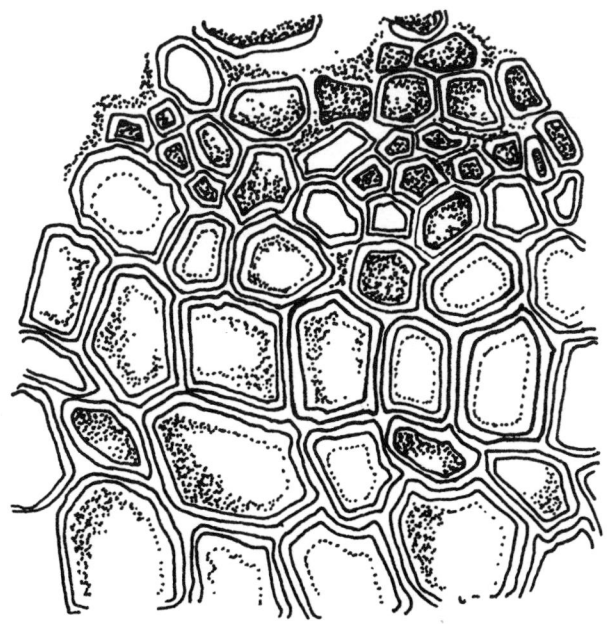

2 You will see from the diagram on this page how similar the cross sections are to the linked loop construction of knitting.

3 If the sample is to be used for garment decoration, then the size, background fabric, yarns and threads must be considered carefully. However, for a framed picture the requirements are not so vital.

4 Disco, party or evening wear allows the use of fancy yarns, the lights creating interesting shadows and glitter.

5 Firstly, prepare the background fabric – this is an important part of the design, so suitable fabric should be selected and prepared. There is plenty of scope for experimentation.

6 Cut a piece of fine white cotton 25 cm × 25 cm. Batik this sample using the spot technique, or tie-dye it. Then dye it in a colour similar in tone to the metallic yarn you have chosen to use. Allow to dry, then remove the wax or string – see pages 9 and 15.

7 Stretch the prepared background fabric in an embroidery ring.

8 Prepare the knitted sample by:

    casting on 20 stitches
    knit 7 rows in garter stitch
    8th row – knit 8 stitches then drop a loop
    knit 6 stitches then drop a loop
    knit 1 row
    cast off.

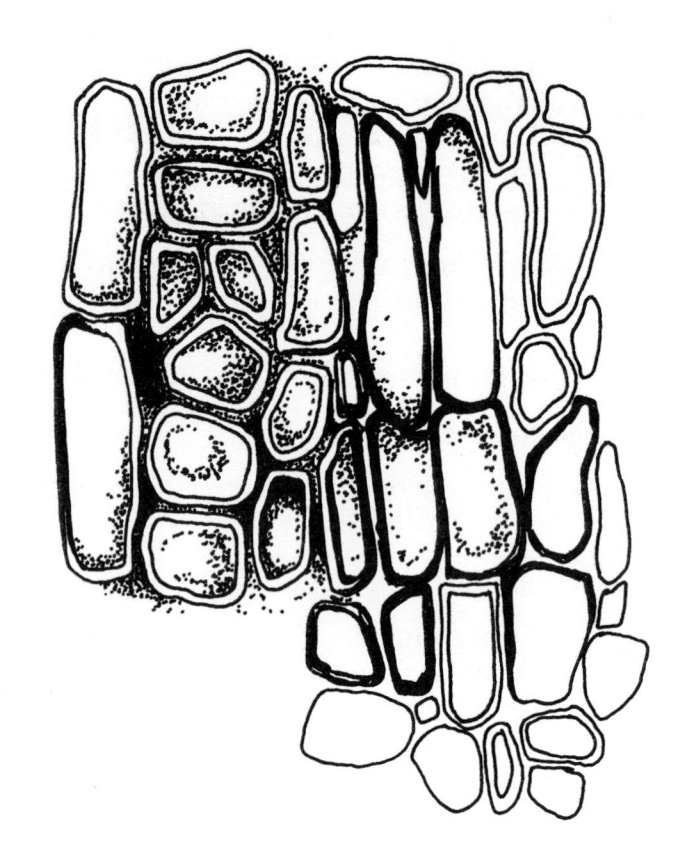

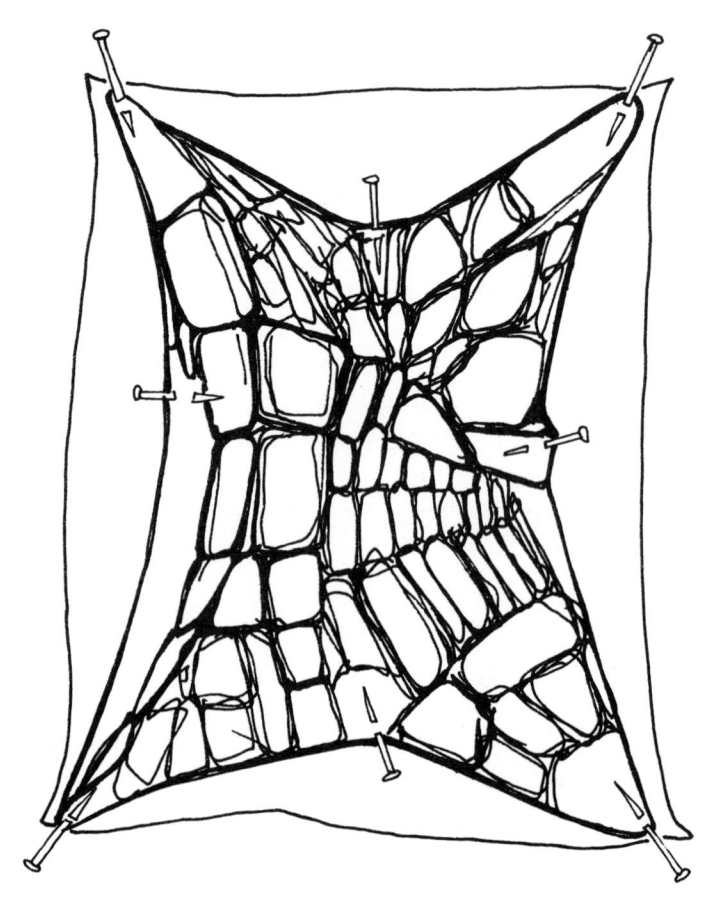

9 Pin the sample to the background fabric – stretching, manipulating and distorting it to open up the knitting – see diagram.

10 Attach the sample to the background fabric. This can be done by couching or machine embroidery.

11 When the knitted sample is fixed in place, further small pieces of texture can be added e.g. small beads, sequins or hand sewn stitches. Great care is needed when developing the design in this way so that each part adds something to the whole. The design can easily become over-elaborate, overbalanced and confused.

12 Remove the design from the embroidery ring and adapt it for its purpose. The diagrams give you some suggestions that you could incorporate into garments you make.

13 An alternative to this idea is to attach the knitted sample to two thicknesses of fabric. The top one must be firm so that it does not distort, both fabrics must be of suitable texture and colour. Stretch the fabrics and attach the knitting. Then cut out of the top fabric some of the shapes between the stretched loops to reveal the lower fabric. The larger the hole, the stronger the edge should be.

This design lends itself to this technique.

Project 3 Pebbles and pools – a decorative textile hanging

Points to consider before starting the project:

> The purpose of this project is to produce a fabric hanging that is a combination of crafts and techniques.
> How many different crafts and techniques do you feel confident in using?
> Would they be applicable to this project?

Suggested uses:

> part decoration for a tourist information office
> suitable product for a craft shop
> decoration for any living room, lounge or office

Draw up a design brief considering the following:

> production of sketches, designs and drawings
> suitable fabrics and decoration for background fabric
> available fabrics, yarns and threads
> colour, sizes, cost
> production of patterns

Suggested size: 40 cm × 45 cm

Suggested fabric:

> white cotton 40 cm × 45 cm
> dyes and equipment for tie-dye or batik – optional
> a selection of fabrics, yarns (textured) and embroidery cottons
> knitting needles
> thread rings and pieces of cut lace – optional

Working hints

It is not really necessary to do preparatory sketches and designs to create an image of water and pebbles. This is an opportunity to work directly with the background fabric to create the effect of flowing water. Explore and experiment with different techniques such as batik, tie-dye and smocking.

1 You could applique the background using suitable coloured and textured fabrics. Cut the fabrics and arrange directly onto the background fabric before attaching them by hand-stitching or machine-stitching.

2 Examine some rocks and pebbles. Make a note of the colours and textures, then find suitable yarn in which to interpret the surface of the pebble.

3 Every pebble is different, some smooth and almost round, others rough and angular. Follow this simple pattern to knit a pebble in the appropriate colour and texture:

> cast on 4
> knit 1 row
> next row increase 1 stitch at each end
> knit 1 row
> next row increase 1 stitch at each end
> knit 4 rows
> next row increase 2 stitches at each end
> knit 7 rows
> you should now have 16 stitches
> knit 7 rows
> next row decrease 2 stitches at each end of the row
> knit 1 row
> next row decrease 2 stitches at each end of the row
> knit 1 row
> cast off

Repeat the pattern for the other half of the pebble. Sew together with the right sides inside leaving a small opening for stuffing. Turn right side out and sew up the hole.

4 Now draft your own patterns for pebbles by simply changing the number of stitches you cast on, increase, decrease etc. Try changing your yarn and size of needles. The number of pebbles you knit depends upon the amount of time you have and the design you have chosen.

5 Some pebbles can be made from coloured felt, or other suitable fabric, with texture embroidered on one side only before they are stuffed. Try using clusters of french knots, satin stitch, or cut parts from old lace curtains and attaching them with simple embroidery stitches. Threaded rings attached with different embroidery cottons can also give an imaginative and creative surface to the pebble – see diagram.

6 Sew the knitted and three-dimensional pebbles firmly onto the background fabric.

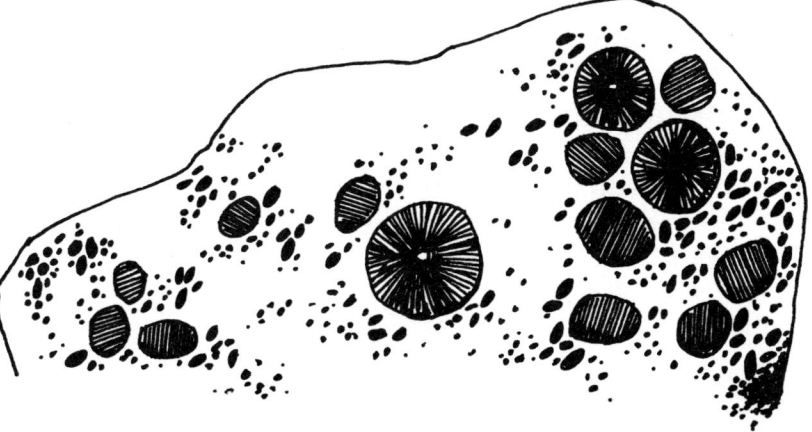

Questions

1 Make a list of as many items as you can which can be hand knitted.

2 Give reasons why many hand-knitted garments are still produced. Sketch a few examples of some hand-knitted items.

3 Which of the following are types of wool? –

   mohair, Arran, lycra, herdwick, chenille, Shetland, jersey.

4 Draw a design for a sweater based on the idea of "Licorice Allsorts".

5 What is the difference between warp and weft knitting?

6 What are the three main sources of fibres from which yarns are made?

7 List the main stitches used in knitting.

8 Place your hand (with the fingers apart) on a sheet of paper and draw around it. Imagine this was the pattern for a child's pair of gloves. Create an imaginative design onto the shape using one of the following themes:

   zoo animals
   happy families
   stripes – limit the number of colours you use to 6.

Tasks for further study

1 Draw the pure wool symbol and the wash care label, then describe in detail how a woollen sweater should be washed.

2 Merino sheep produce the best wool. Find out where the breed originated and why the wool is superior.

3 Kaffe Fassett is a designer/knitter. His work is a superb blend of colour and pattern. The designs are based on simple shapes and stocking stitch. Find out more about his work and sketch two of the garments he has designed.

4 Knitting is one method of fabric construction. Describe in detail, with the aid of diagrams, other ways in which fabric can be constructed.